Alake Shilling

The Hippest Trip in America
By Land, Air & Sea

Alake Shilling

Jeffrey Deitch Pacific

A River, a Petal or a Paw

Laura Owens

In her paintings and sculptures, Alake Shilling captures stillness in motion and, through this seeming contradiction, creates a world populated by humanlike animals, flowers, and insects brimming with emotion. A bristling animus is evident everywhere in these works. Even landscapes and still lifes become anthropomorphized portraits. The paint jiggles before our eyes, and so do the creatures it depicts. Limbs throb. Eyes quiver, as if about to shed a tear. Paint, solidified mid-pour, mirrors these creatures, teeming with life, even in moments of repose.

Shilling likes her creatures plump and vibrating. Tigers, bunnies, and frogs are trembling with vitality. We can't help but make a mental bridge, a psychic squeeze; we empathize. The connection feels truer than our typical response to a portrait because these works mirror the familiar human state of having at least three conflicting feelings at once. A painting or sculpture by Shilling is replete with recognition. Terrified, in love, and angry? Nauseous, titillated, and scared? Language is always insufficient to explain.

What should be cloying and too much never is; it's contained ecstasy within a dirty and slippery world. Imperfect, and not ever just "happy," like in *Froggy Guy Stepping on the B-Guy* (2018), there is some conflict, and it's not clear where the play is ending and the pain is beginning. These works are messy, imperfect, round, squeezable, edible, explosive, and jittery. Shilling's paintings and sculptures are filled with joy and everything that accompanies that feeling.

The world she creates mimics the paintings' own explosive making. We are standing in front of Action painting mid-moment. Splashes or splurts are felt like onomatopoetic gestures that hover deftly between representing an idealized glom of color and the physical reality of the actual paint pooled on the canvas. The forms are inflated and round. There's a billowy flatness, like puffy stickers, a tactile quality that makes painting feel quilted, brocaded, and bejeweled. Texture differentiates space. In an interview with Anthony Valdez, Shilling alludes to the great emotional attachment people have to texture. Textures moving us through not only depth of field but also emotional resonance; differences felt sensually in the brain as we access them only by scanning a picture at a distance.

The paintings move between abstract compositions and an atmospheric world of sprightly dancing forms that are sometimes recognizable, even familiar. And yet, this is not a flat, candyland, front-of-house face; this is the real "them," unvarnished and behind the scenes. These anthropomorphized gestures are

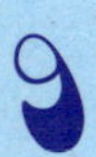

present with all their emotions, their memories, and their futures. We have the sense that these forms are passing, just like we are, through troubled worlds. We see their literalness in the painted surface, and phantasmagoric inspirations born of color and texture make their being-ness temporary and special. We are lucky to meet them in the flesh. How do you do? What's happening today? Oh really? Do tell! Their interests guide us through the painting, their world. They have sent the invitation; we stand half in and out of a threshold.

Shilling smartly breaks the frame to put us in the picture. Look closely and notice that most of the paintings extend beyond the edge of the canvas, creeping into the world of the gallery where the work is hanging. Paint dries and is allowed to puddle and harden into shapes that weave their way out of the window of painting into our space in the gallery. Thick globs of paint are both part of the depicted scene—for example, a river, petal, or paw—and a reminder of the facticity of paint itself as it sets out on a journey across the canvas. Her work reminds me of a Raphael-designed tapestry that hangs in the halls of the Vatican. In the tapestry, the resurrected Christ emerges from his tomb—depicted as a flat black rectangle on the wall—by stepping out onto a slab with a strong perspectival effect. The figure breaks the frame of the tomb's entrance in a way that pushes him out, away from the picture plane. You feel like he is stepping off the wall, his foot about to land on your head. And he's happy to emerge after death, alive, metaphorically ready to dance. Shilling's pictures do this same dance. We are invited to join—just as her works protrude off the wall, we are correspondingly pulled into their world. Each object is breathing, looking, being, and the painting itself as a whole must catapult itself from this wall: an entranced 3-D spectacular vision. Shilling's works seem to yearn for connection with the viewer, yet I am confident they are complete without me. They're an internal metropolis of emotions, brimming with contradictory impulses, and ready to hug, pounce, or bounce.

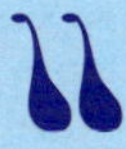

Shilling's show at 356 Mission was one of the last before the gallery's closing and one of the most important. There was an energy around her and her work that gave everyone working at the gallery an urgent desire to make the exhibition happen. The opportunity to introduce her work to a wider Los Angeles audience was one of 356 Mission's great pleasures.

My Time With Alake Shilling

Grant Levy-Lucero

I'll never forget my first time meeting Alake. It was the summer of 2016, and I had just begun to find my groove at Clay Day, an open ceramic workshop facilitated by Laura Owens at 356 Mission. I was about a year into my ceramic practice at this point and had just begun to arrive at the technique and forms that most people know me for today. I had received our weekly Clay Day announcement, but this one was from our new host, signed only as "Alake."

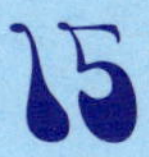

There were a lot of artists that I had met coming through 356 Mission at that time, but Alake was someone I had never heard of. Eager to make a good impression and ingratiate myself to the new Clay Day host, I decided to arrive extra early. I walked right up to her and said, "Hi, I'm Grant. You must be A Lake." I think we were both a bit embarrassed when she politely corrected me, "No, I'm Alake! And I know you, you're Grant, and you're super famous." I was a bit confused as I don't think I'm famous at all, but truthfully, I was also flattered. I knew right then we would be fast friends, and it didn't take long for our friendship to flourish.

Like most, the first thing I noticed about Alake was her voice—a mix of childlike wonderment and unbridled enthusiasm exudes from every sentence. I think, like most of the world, that Alake has created her voice can be a telling feature of how she sees herself and her work. At once saccharin and sweet, but after you listen and observe, only then do the somber undertones become apparent.

I often find myself thinking about the world that Alake has created for herself. A mix of themes and motifs are instantly recognizable to any child of the nineties, with its Lisa Frank Fantasy and Sanrio cast of characters. It's a world built on play and amusement, easy on the eyes and open for all who care to approach it. It's within this world that Alake feels comfortable expressing some of the more difficult topics that the work tackles. Depression and loneliness are common themes buried under the groovy waves or radiant fields of flowers. It's this dichotomy that I have found so inspiring in my friendship with Alake. The paintings and sculptures she creates are a genuine extension of her as a person.

Our friendship is one of my most cherished; I truly do not have another connection with anyone like I have with Alake. Sometimes it feels like a big brother/little sister relationship, as I consider Alake part of my family, and she knows I will always have her back. Over the years, we have had the chance to work side by side for many hours, and it has been a real pleasure to have her there to bounce ideas off of and be supported by someone with such unbridled creativity.

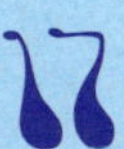

Since my studio is only about a quarter-mile away from her house, it has been a convenient place for her to continue the sculpture side of her practice once our beloved Clay Day and 356 Mission finished. We carved out a little corner for her to feel free to work however she wanted, and it has been amazing to see the works develop and progress. I remember in the beginning days of Clay Day, a ladybug Alake had made was no bigger than the palm of my hand. It was one of the most wonderful works I had seen— it radiated so much joy and was made with such care and love. As time has progressed, it has been amazing to see Alake really sharpen her ability with the material. Not only has the scale grown, but so has her experimentation with colors and glaze. Satins and metallics, sunbursts and sparkles have all given her a new creative lease that she explores with much amusement.

In this way, I have found Alake's presence to be a huge inspiration. Her free-wielding, creative, and inventive spirit works in sharp contrast to my daily ritual of regimented studio practice. Many days, I find myself envious of her ability to create without the pressures that impact me—oftentimes

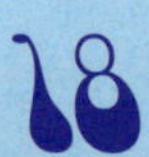

choosing to make work for absolutely no end goal other than her pure love of it and satisfaction in the expression of it. In our ever-present visual culture, with the pressure to always be working toward the next show or fair, it is extremely refreshing to have an artist like Alake, who couldn't care less about being seen at the "cool" opening or getting the right introduction to further her own professional agenda.

But don't mistake this for an overall under-appreciation for the finer things. Alake has an acute vision for her own personal style, a sharp curatorial eye on the high-fashion stylings of big fashion brands and handmade indie designers alike. The same can be said for her taste in music, food, and, yes, other art, too. She may play with passive indifference in public, but she has a well-trained eye/ear/mouth, knowing what she likes, and a strong aesthetic argument as to why what she likes is "good."

Any story of Alake would be incomplete without mention of her mother, Kidogo Kennedy. If you happen to see Alake in public, there is a strong

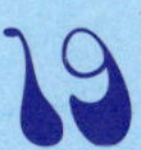

chance that you will also see Kidogo. One conversation with Kidogo, and it is obvious how much love and support Alake was raised with. Kidogo often shares stories of baby Alake sitting in the corner making drawings for hours, finding the ability to entertain herself with her artistic ambitions at such a young age. It's clear that Alake's world building escapism has been decades in the making, and the stories she's created have deep roots in their family.

I'd like to return to the work here for a moment, specifically, the ceramic sculptures. Many days, upon Alake's arrival, I will ask her what she plans to start making. She will normally ask me my opinion of what animal I think she should start on—a turtle, dog, snake, bug, butterfly, or something along those lines (I usually always say dog). What transpires after that is nothing short of amazing. She starts at the base and works her way up, coiling and smoothing, cutting and shaping, only pulling away for a singular lunch break. She finds the zone and completes her vision with obsessive focus. Adding shapes and extrusions, sanding off bits here and there. By the end, something so elementary as a

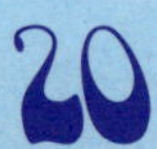

"dog" has been rendered expertly in her world: exuding her personality and characteristics until it has become another in the long line of her cast of characters. The way she is able to take a material as rudimentary as clay and turn it into a personified character, with a complete backstory and its own place in the world, is the magic of Alake.

You or I might set off to make a dog sculpture in all earnestness and probably get pretty close to rendering a family pet or the pet of a friend. Alake is able to create it with its own story—something like Doby, the dog, who is best friends with the turtle and off on an adventure to find true love on a cross-country road trip by train, plane, and car. If the dog looks a little forlorn, it's because the car broke down and all seems lost, but they've still got their best clothes on and will have a good time no matter what. It's this magical thinking and ability to create such a rich narrative that makes Alake really shine. By inviting us into this private world of hers, she is letting us glimpse all her vulnerabilities.

I don't think she's ever been fully comfortable sharing her own work. As much as we all love it,

I don't think she is ever entirely satisfied with her own creations. Almost all the artists I know struggle with feelings of insecurities in their own work. Alake has such a deeply personal connection to all of her work, it feels like giving away an actual part of herself. Like a phantom limb or piece of her soul, her exhibitions are a deeply generous offering to the public. Sure, we can all familiarize ourselves with images of any given artist's work on Instagram or online, but once you walk into an actual exhibition, the vision of the artist can truly live. This is where her voice can be heard the loudest, and spending so much time creating the world for her characters to live in requires an obsessive follow-through to ensure everyone is given the proper space for each story to be told. Keeping this in mind, it's clear why we may catch a glimpse of her work out in the world with such rarity, and any such experience should be viewed as a gift.

I consider myself very lucky to have had the opportunity to collaborate with Alake on a piece for the exhibition *Clay Pop*, curated by Alia Dahl at Jeffrey Deitch in the fall of 2021. It came about very naturally during our time working together.

The conversation started as a desire to collaborate, and after a brief brainstorm, we thought of either a shelled creature with one of my forms on the back or one of my pieces with one of her characters hanging on the side. We arrived at Aesop's fable of "The Tortoise and the Hare," but with some funk on it: one of her characters, Shelly Turtle, and one of my pieces, with a hand-painted version of Trix cereal with its whacky rabbit placed on top. What resulted was one of my favorite pieces I've ever worked on. We had so much fun, and I found our collaboration to be smooth and natural—our two voices joining together to tell one of the world's most well-known stories.

Knowing Alake has been one of the greatest pleasures of my life. It's been with great admiration and joy that I have been able to support her and her practice as she grows and pushes her creations further and further. She is one of the smartest, most creative, and most talented people I have ever encountered, always thoughtful and measured in her opinion and expression of it. Her friendship is a gift to anyone who has had the opportunity to sit with her and trade ideas. Her abundant enthusiasm and excitement for creating are infectious, and you can't help but feel genuinely blessed to encounter it. I hope I've done a good job explaining how magical Alake is and how rare of a personality she has. It has been a real honor to do so.

Alake's Laboratory

Permana Nazif

Alake Shilling lives in a pink-castle house with stained-glass windows and blush-colored flower bushes framing her laboratory-like studio. Most times I've been there, lightly tapping the knocker to the doorbell's chime and peering through the mini window-flap in the door, Alake greets me in an identically rosy outfit with a jazzy hat and her winged, caterpillar-like eyeglasses. We share a deep appreciation for sweets and caffeine. The house, save for the studio with its astringent and acrid elixirs, ordinarily smells akin to the pastries I bring for us—as if sugarplum butterflies and gingerbread teddy bears donning Kiko Kostadinov and eighties Zucca attire frequently lunch with Alake. Often, I'm surprised not to find mountains of glitter as flooring while color-changing vapor glides between the books of Op art and piles of rocks and minerals, up to the precious trinkets and bric-a-brac of donnish frogs or porcelain hamburgers, coating each and everything it comes into contact with in a fine sugary dust. The atmosphere unfailingly seeps through the alchemical if not magical in Alake's studio, particularly when dotted with her sculptural paintings that are quite materially larger than—I'd say, human—life in content and form.

But to "once upon a time" and continue through to "Happily ever after" exclusively with magic and the surreal from a vacuous nowhere would be extremely naive. Alake's nonpareil imagination is informed by equal parts research and improvised experimentation. An Alake bibliography at this particular moment would range from TV sitcom set designs to field guides and zoology books. Lately, she's been experimenting with nail art and talking to nail technicians—constantly expanding and debunking the limiting parameters and boring normative of what "art" is. The otherworldly solvents and glops of nail art transfer onto the ethereal textures of Alake's canvases, making new with what "press-on" nail art can presage. Apparently, certain nail technologies are only available for certified nail technicians, hence Alake's experimental, wandering path—one... that is neither aimless nor inhabiting a pure and purposeless form.

On my most recent visit, scattered around the glue and spackling paste for the paintings' hefty yet viscous-seeming borders, were various bottles of nail polish. The still-in-progress papier-mâché substructure of the funky perimeter seemed as if it had broken open like a piñata, where candies had fallen out out, multicolored like the nail polish bottles around us. Bearing resemblance to the undefined black substance named Chemical X in cult 1990s animated television series *The Powerpuff*

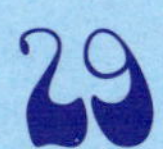

Girls, the spunky-colored, iridescent nail polishes were a far cry from the cartoon theme song's initial distress and abjection of the *je ne sais quoi*-X. The sublime that is most associated with X gives way not only in nameless colors (how can one objectively name the color that is life? That is pizzazz? That is melancholy?) but also to subject matter such as the notorious, simultaneously charming and yet weighed-down eyes that are painted onto most of Alake's various characters. In *The End of the Road...Only God Knows Where We'll Go* (2021), Jolly Bear, a gloved bear, steers a train with the same worried tulip-lidded eyes. Neither conductor nor locomotive look forward, but instead wayward, with furrowed lids. We don't need to theorize the mutual constitution of cute and beauty with horror and distress to indicate the worry these creatures embody and the non-progression (of, also, Modernity, duh). We can see it in their eyes. Or at the abrupt end of their tracked path that runs into grass where movement will be, foreseeably, stalled. The magenta hearts shooting out of the train's whistle or exhaust and the multicolored sparkle-stoned

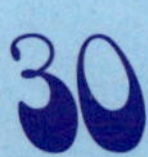

cave they have just come out of don't offer relief from the stress.

It's a brilliant amalgamation of sugar, spice, and everything nice, with the additional ingredient of Chemical X. Unlike Professor Utonium of *The Powerpuff Girls*, however, Alake Shilling's concoctions fold in this Chemical X with intention. What exactly is Chemical X? For the young Powerpuff girl superheroes, X is part of their chemical makeup, accidentally dumped into the birthing cauldron by their father-scientist-creator. X marks the effervescent intersection between cuteness on the one side and violence, power, horror, and the science-fictional on the other. X could be what makes them super- or, extra-human. It's where the seemingly contradictory can reside, surfacing tensions that contract and expand, destabilize, and, eventually, articulate. Both "V" sides of the X, supposedly antagonistic, secrete one another, make one another, make love—that separation as a not-in-between being nothing. Surrounded by pungent paints, glitters, and polishes that could well be

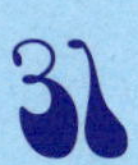

singeing and frothing test tubes and beakers, Alake's improvised experimentations hiss and bubble with the mercurial and elusive X.

Utonium's mistake is Alake's intent. X is the intersection of the matrixial within the mapped folds or even the break. A speculative space opens up with X that de/refolds consistently and constantly. The fold, the break, the X is not a neutral space—Alake marks its possibility for a beyond. She paints in the liminal. Unlike the Powerpuff girls, who occupy very particular, racial, if not gender and sex-order aesthetics, identities, and, thus, histories, Alake's X does not reinscribe racialized and gendered representational discursives and, thus, mater(eal)ialities. Instead, these works operate within new Universal conceptions of being, as re-lational to femininity, cuteness, and expansive emotional states. Frankly, X marks the spot. And that spot is cute for cute's sake.

It's like the nostalgic affect of much of Alake's works that ends in confused disorientation: these are not, in fact, mythologized characters familiar from

our childhood memories, but instead an occupation of the real and the speculative. The gloved hands on Jolly Bear look similar to a particular animated mouse's hands, while the train's face resembles a certain blue steam engine I grew up watching. Thomas and Mickey, however, never indicated that only god knows where we will go. There was always a linear trajectory, with a defined beginning, middle, and end—in that order. The painting isn't necessarily Postmodern either. Here, Modernism doesn't make its way into Postmodernism. Mickey never gets to be meme-ified.

In fact, Alake's work is a lot like the artist herself—cute, silly, loving, and iconic. She keeps it sweet but has a good BS detector. She occupies the world, as does her work, in nonnormative ways that should be aspired to collectively. Every "Cool beans" and "Gee, golly" she utters is critical, and with style. She knows that the bear and train could be very well done for. That knowledge is not unlike her keen sense of substandard culture writing and decorative social niceties (a "buttering up," as Alake calls them) that prioritize the vapid and trendy. Her work isn't necessarily glitter-coating everything. The glitter, in fact, lends itself to various degrees of opacity and exposure, overlapping and intersecting with one another, where truth can surface. I mean, quite literally, the glitter nail polish she uses congeals the glitter by way of transparent polish. And this is the genius of Alake Shilling: dense theoretical concepts, tangled and wrapped into readymades, overdeterminations parsed through glitter that many of us can understand on an affective level. She's Alchemical Shilling!

Her methodology, a folding that unfolds and refolds simultaneously, echoes improvisatory aestheticized forms. Chance and coincidence are prioritized with spontaneity, leading the way in all directions, which somehow merge with each other, enfold and detach at various X points that operate as transference structures of aesthetic content. These X structures are the sublime Chemical X in Alake's mixture of Flashe paint or nail polish. As non-formulaic and mercurial, they trouble normative and linear conditions of the production of (aesthetic) meaning. If we take Professor Utonium's name to be derived from nuclear-weapon-producing Plutonium, Alake's works quite literally blow up any standardized aesthetic content, thus, also meaning, production. The cuteness (*qt*-ness included) is only created with the horrific. The mutual constitution of the two is also simultaneously formed via a lack of the one in the other.

In Alake's world, therefore, sand is used to make water. Sand, along with paint, glue, and the—naturally—waterproof sealant caulk, textures the frothy finish and dynamics of ocean water in many of her paintings. In *Major Wave* (2021), a nonchalant dolphin named Splash rides majestic, grooving waves, unbothered by the celestial landscape. Sand-made sea foam splaying and bordering the canvas gushes out with sprinkled stars and hearts while Splash is consumed by the painted curls of their namesake. Splash may or may not be immune to the bewitching curl of the waves, where apathy is hard to distinguish from the sedation. And it is this need to enforce or name the binary that Alake blurs. She and I have talked about the perversity of nature-show narrations at length. Her stance on the subjective (as in discriminatory, as in nonobjective) voice-over in a purported "documentary" or "nonfictional" TV show is quite clear through her use of the indefinite in the content matter of her artworks. Deep, masculinized voices, as if from the godly above, describing-as-fact a crested gecko as the conniving villain, set to dissonant sounds, bear no weight in Alake's world. Expectations are destabilized. Sand can make water instead of delimiting what is and is not. The octopus in *Tell Me Another Joke* (2021) isn't vilified for eating the terrified fish circling it. Think of Tweety and Jerry's eternal struggle with their feline friends, Sylvester and Tom. One fish caught in the octopus's tentacle, in fact, is cannibalistic. When I ask about it, Alake calls it as it is: life isn't easy under the sea. I mean, it's the circle of life. Bubbles, the circular formation of the octopus's tentacles, the mouths, the puffy fish: they reinforce the orbit. Maybe the X morphs into an O—the fantastical sublime is at hand in Alake's work and this wouldn't be a far stretch—into the embrace of the XO as much as the emoticon it figures horizontally.

Following Alake herself and her hand are trails of
these XOs. That zest and blooming, popping hearts
that trail lend themselves to the haptic quality of
her work. To snuggle with it, to taste (the piquant),
to pet, to hold, to dip in, to adore. To know Alake's
work is, infinitely, to love.

"I Came into the World to Bring You Color"
—Alake Shilling, 1994

Kidogo Kennedy

Art is an ebullient tool Alake Shilling has utilized to explore her understanding of creation. Over time, she has developed a language rich with texture and invention to interrogate human emotion in a full expression of herself. Her paintings and ceramics are a cacophony of ideas, thoughts, and experiences standing on the edge of a glittered baroque frenzy, anchored by unadulterated Black girl swag. Alake beckons us to interact and analyze the world in her language.

PINNACLE MOMENTS IN TIME

Alake sat in her stroller, eyes big as saucers, intently watching me rifle through a rounder of dresses. I turned to her smiling as I held a long black dress against my frame and said, "Do you like it?" She slowly shook her head no, and I could barely contain my laughter. "You don't?" I asked. "Why not?" She reached out and grabbed a linen maxi dress. "I like this one." All I could do was smile, grab the garment, and head for the counter. The dress was bubble-gum pink.

She climbed into the backseat of our red Dodge hatchback, looking as if she had a huge secret. "How was your day at school, doll?" Her response was a dazzling smile. As I drove, I noticed her hand securely shoved deep into the right pocket of her favorite denim overalls. I looked at her face from time to time in the rearview mirror, pondering her look of sheer satisfaction. Usually, after a day in the sandbox, the first thing she wanted once we arrived home to wash her hands. I stood at the sink waiting for her to climb onto her tiny step stool and was astonished when she refused to soap her hands. I carefully pried her tightly balled fist open as a flurry of tears began streaming down her little, exasperated face. "It's mine; it's mine!" she stammered, slowly opening her hand. There was only the smallest piece of a crayon in her palm. "It's mine," she said, "it's my shiny pink."

As I prepared my belongings to head out the door, the phone rang. It was the sitter calling to say she had an emergency and would not be able to make it. I dashed into the kitchen, placed some red grapes, string cheese, and celery sticks into a few snack bags, and tossed them into Alake's favorite Hello Kitty lunch pail, but before heading toward my school, I stopped at Toys "R" Us to purchase the Big Box of Crayola's. Although I knew bringing a toddler to class was certainly not the university norm, in this instance, I had no choice. Once we arrived on campus, I stopped by the communication studies department and asked the administrative assistant for a few sheets of blank copy paper.

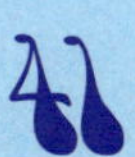

Then I explained: "Doll," I said, "Mother must attend her class, and I will need you to be very quiet. If you make any noise, the professor will ask me to leave." "Whatever you think about or want to say, use the crayons and put it on this paper." "If you get hungry, snacks are in your lunch box." "Today is very important, understand?" She smiled brightly and turned her full attention to the Big Box of Crayola's, as if it were gold. During my class, Alake never uttered one word. At the end, I sat beside her, eager to see what was on the paper. To my delight and amazement, there emerged a vibrant world of flora that bespoke an imaginary, pre-historic, jungle fantasy, brimming with flowers of neon pink, malachite, and xanthic. My eyes were tantalized by mountains of amethyst, rolling emerald hills, and snaking turquoise rivers. I turned to her and asked, "You draw?" She simply batted her long curly eyelashes and beamed.

Pondering Alake Shilling's choice of "becoming" a fine artist often pulls me into a whirlwind of dreamy colors, glitter, and jubilee. She once stated to me,

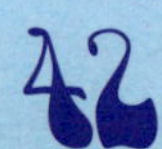

emphatically, "I am different from other kids my age!" "How so?" I queried with a slight smile. "Well," she stated thoughtfully, "other kids must be girls or boys while I get to be an artist!" She continued, "I do not know who I would be if I were not an artist." Later, I quietly stood and watched her playing outside; she laughed with her friends, casually holding her favorite plush toy, lovingly named Baby Lion King, and mulled over our conversation. I felt pleased Alake had the freedom to live outside of a box, and I was eager to see how her feeling of freedom might play out in her life.

As I noticed a technicolor world full of limitless imagination emerge, I hoped art would become an activity vast enough to sustain her interest over the years. So, I watched, nurtured, and encouraged her ingenuity—because of that, she never stopped exploring her creativity. Alake officially declared her intention to become a fine artist in the third grade. A child's magazine languished on the floor of her classroom, and the cover photo happened to be Jeff Koons's *Balloon Dog*. That afternoon, when I

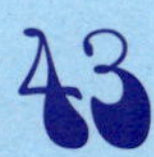

walked into the front room of her school, I scanned the area to locate my joy. I saw her lounging on a coveted beanbag. Usually, she would be sitting there with her eyes trained on the door, waiting for my arrival. However, that day, Alake was intently looking at the cover photo of a magazine perched on her tiny little knees.

Before I could approach, she saw me and readily began the struggle to escape soft corduroy folds of beanbag flesh that cuddled and cushioned her, along with lunch pail and book tote. We met each other in the middle of the room, and her excitement was palpable. Eyes wide as saucers, her glee bubbled in the air like the fleeting euphoria of champagne, making me giddy with delight. I listened with curiosity as Alake clutched the magazine in her hands and began a rant about her treasure. In a nutshell, she thought that dog was amazing! *Balloon Dog* was very much unlike the art I was introducing her to. Up until that point, I was taking her to museums to view the works of Romare Bearden, Jean-Michel Basquiat, Frida Kahlo, Kara Walker, Varnette Honeywood, and Ernie Barnes, whose serious nature did not capture the attention of a butterfly who loved Hello Kitty, Lisa Frank, and Gelly Roll glitter pens.

From the third grade on, Alake's interest in art transformed into an art routine. Today, her practice still follows the same design. First, she plays with paints, or glazes, organizing them into long rows of gradients in each color spectrum, taking her sweet time to discover which color should come first, second, third, and so on. For example, if she is working in green, the big question of the day might be, "Does chartreuse precede or follow lime?" I still quietly watch her moving the mediums back and forth until she is satisfied her color slope from light to dark emerges just right. The result is long lines of perfectly placed paint tubes and jars trailing across the floor of her studio. When her color scheme is complete, Alake begins to draw. I once asked how she decides on subject matter. She smiled and replied, "Oh, it's easy, Mother. I close my eyes, and a mental Rolodex appears." "What is a mental Rolodex?" I asked. She quipped,

"It is a collection of drawings that lives in my head, and I flip through it until I locate a piece I want to create," or "I stare at the blank canvas until something emerges, and I start to draw. It's easy!" she laughed. Finally, Alake's ballet of layering colors and texture begins.

At first, there were just a few splays of glitter here and there, but that experimentation grew into a Hodgepodge of materials mixed and layered until texture was literally spilling off the canvas straight into another world. The first odd material Alake added to paint was a bag of rubber bands. This investigation was followed by sand, flour, shaving cream, rocks, Styrofoam, and any number of items she might identify to satisfy her obsession with touch. At this point, she becomes a scientist investigating how the paint will respond. Pouring the mixture on a blank canvas, she is patient until the concoction dries. Finally, the real magic begins as she completes painting her drawing around and over obstructions, refining haphazard shapes until they align with the scenes Alake explores in her world.

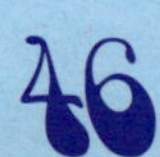

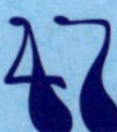

SOURCES

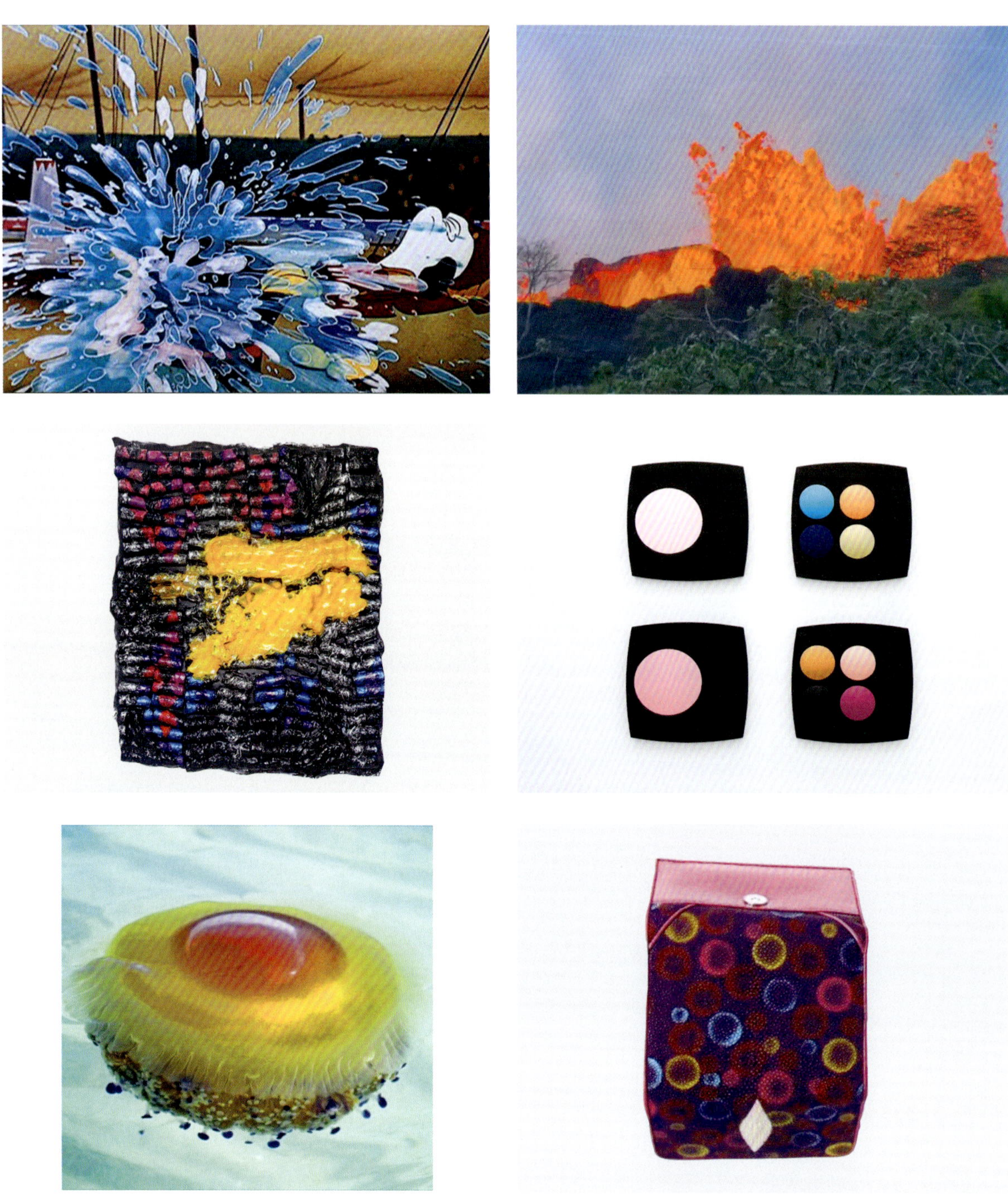

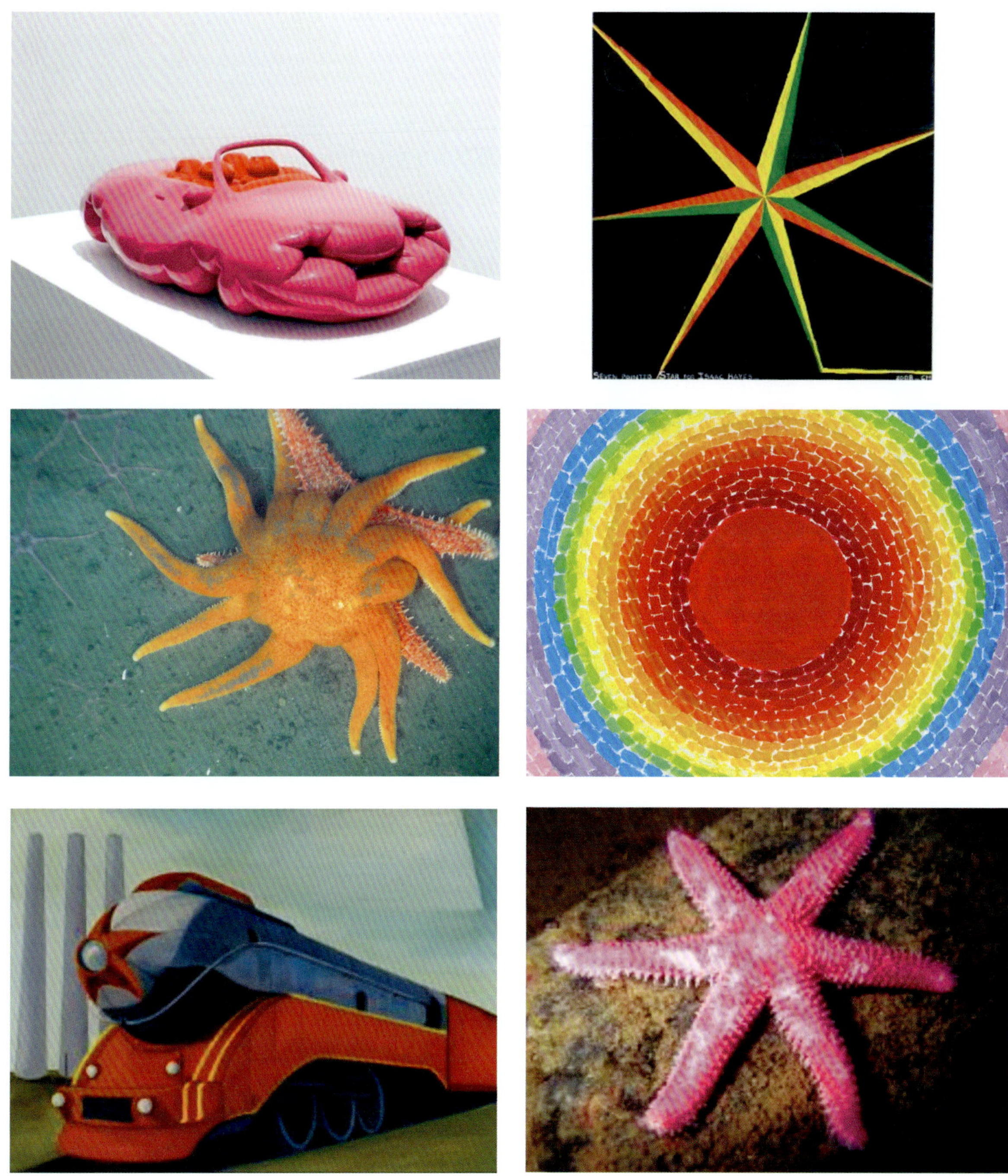

SEVEN POINTED STAR FOR ISAAC HAYES

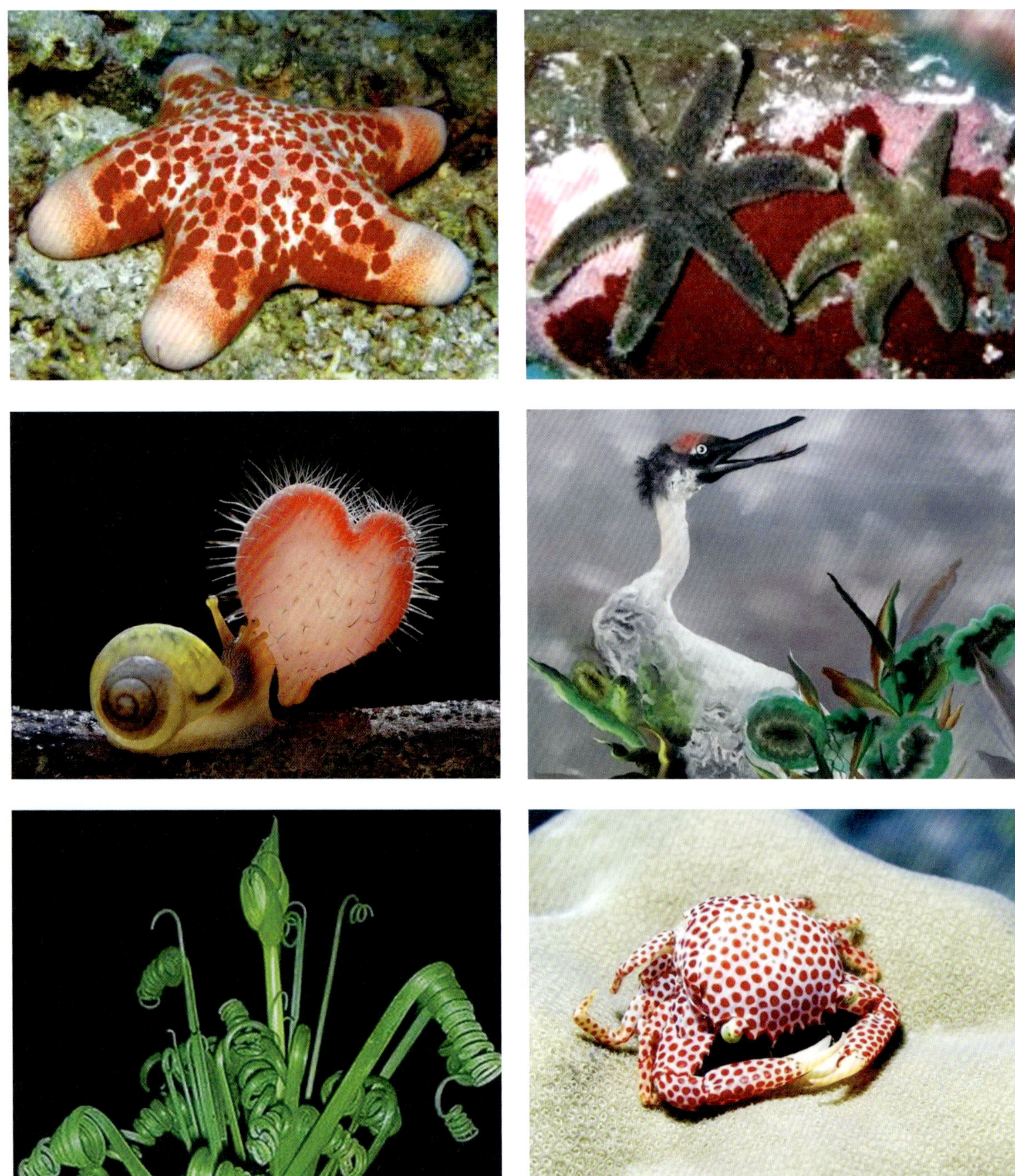

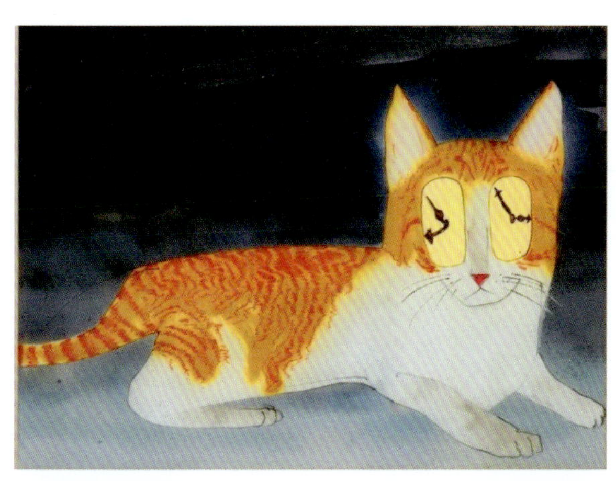
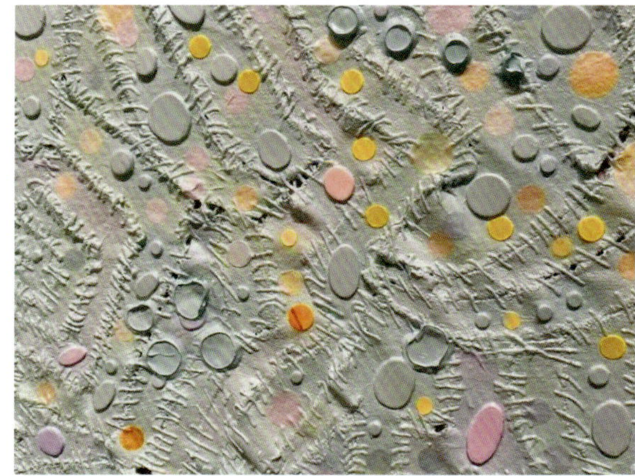
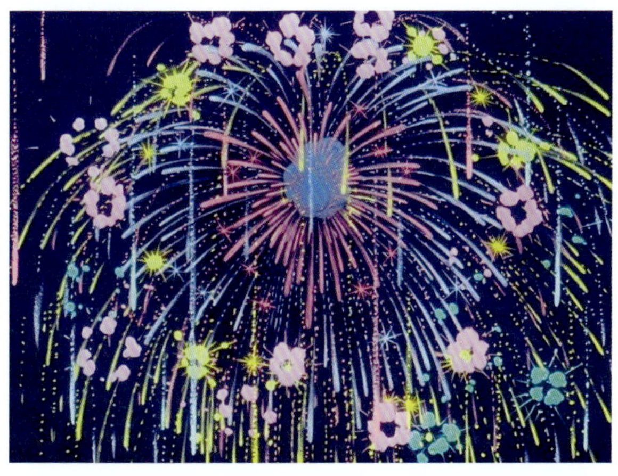
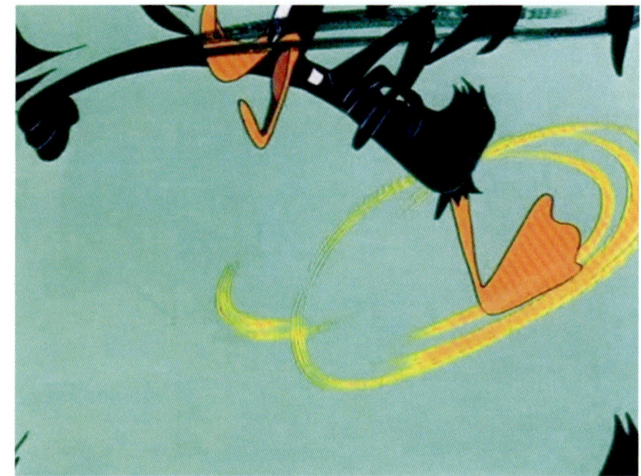
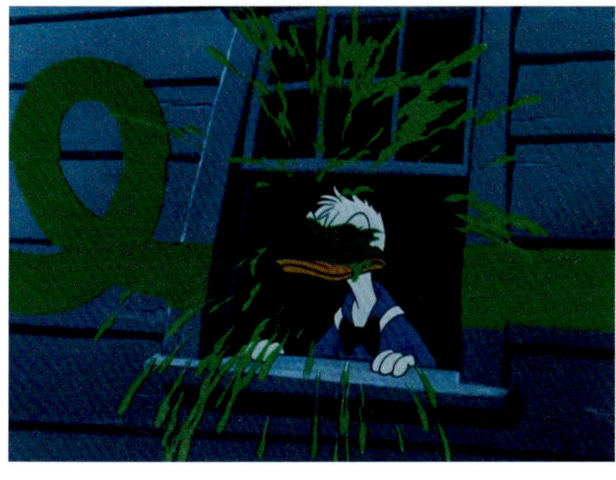
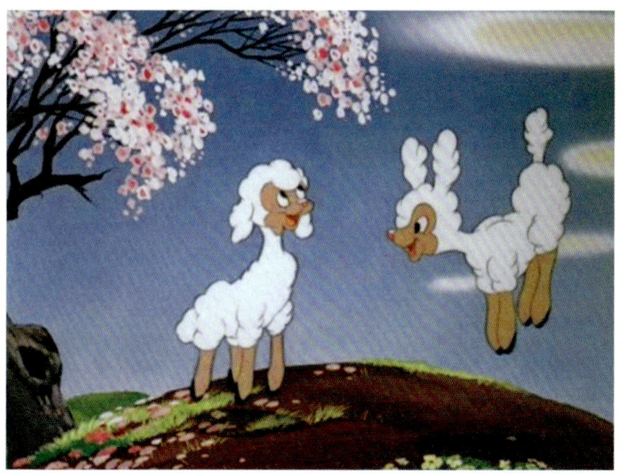

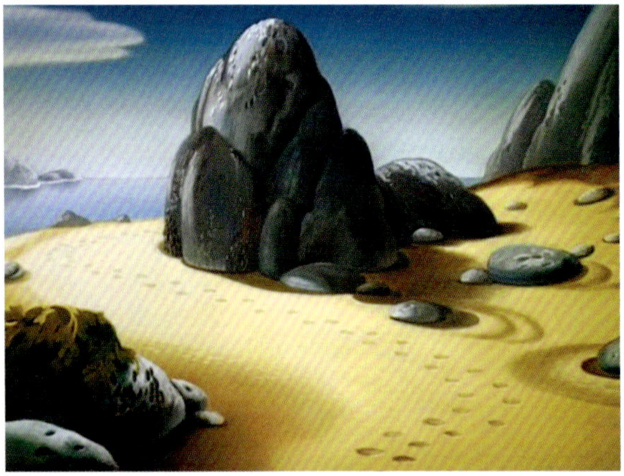

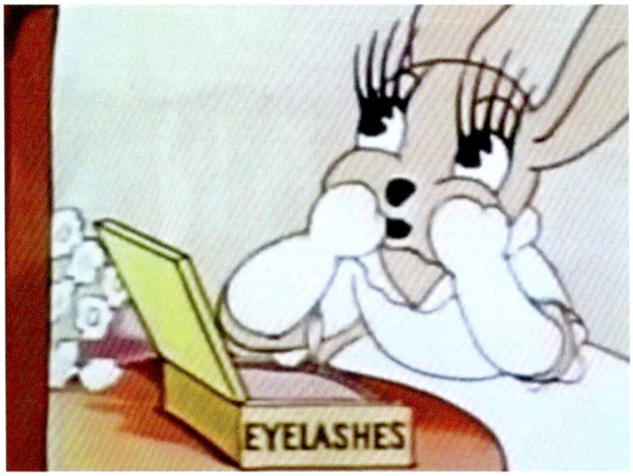

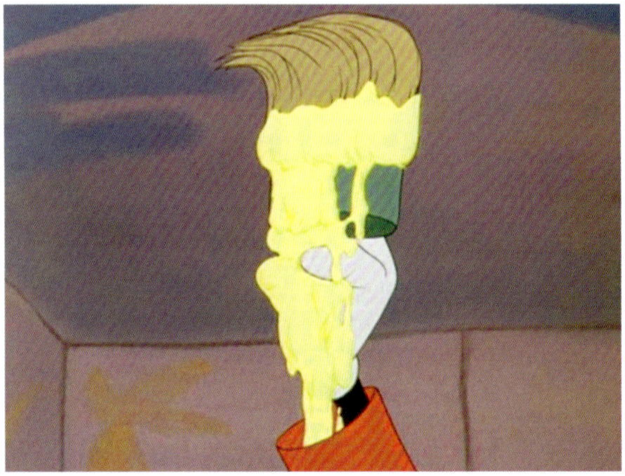

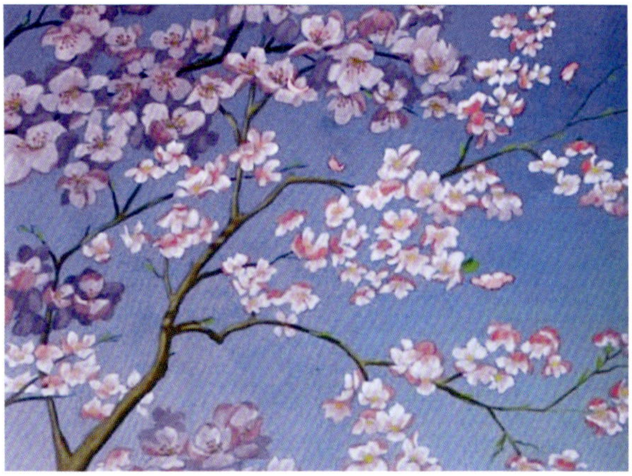

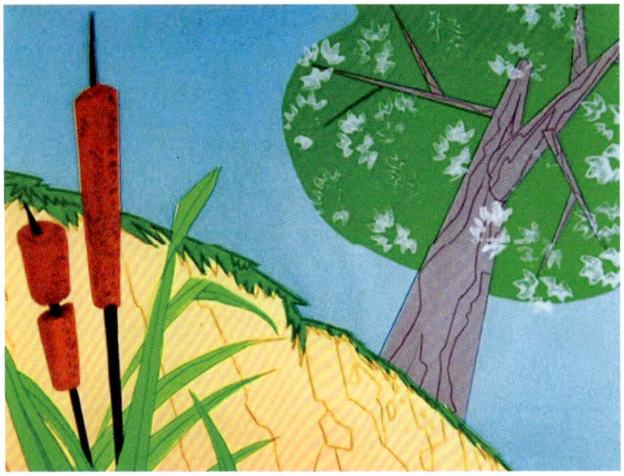

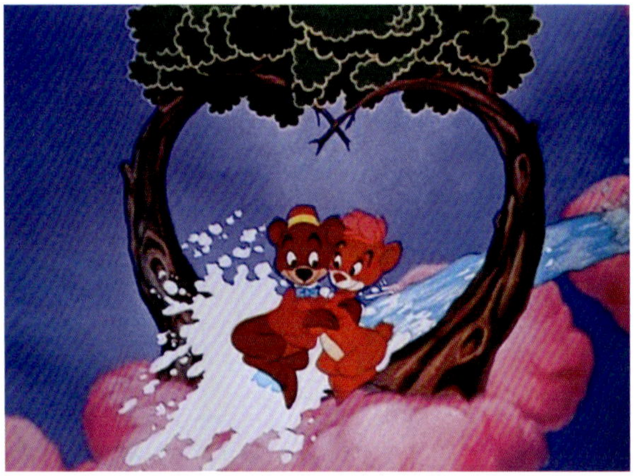

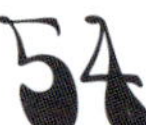

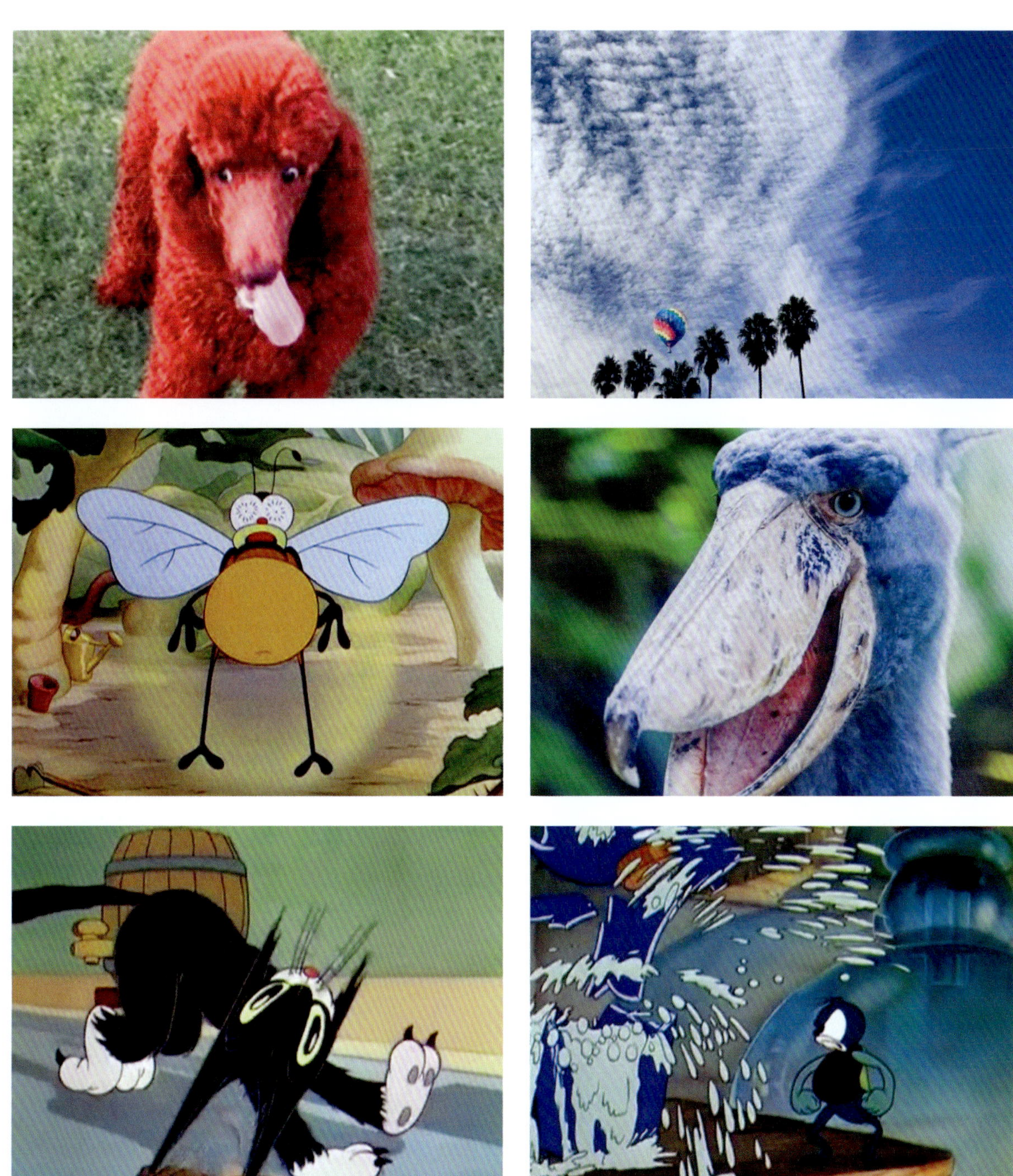

WORKS

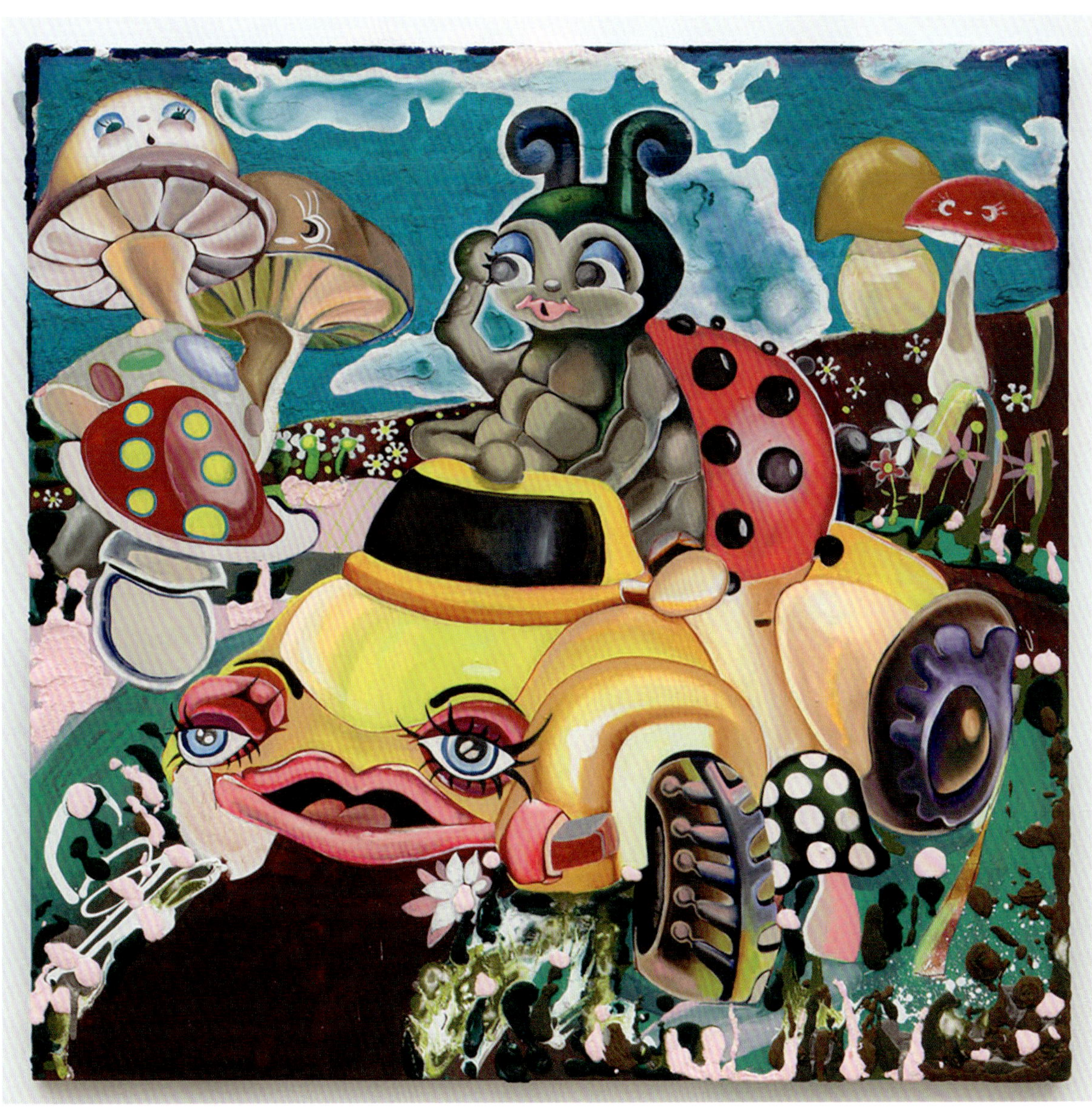

**Tickle Bus is
Back in Town, 2020**

Oil paint, Flashe vinyl paint, sand, and glitter on canvas
60 × 60 inches

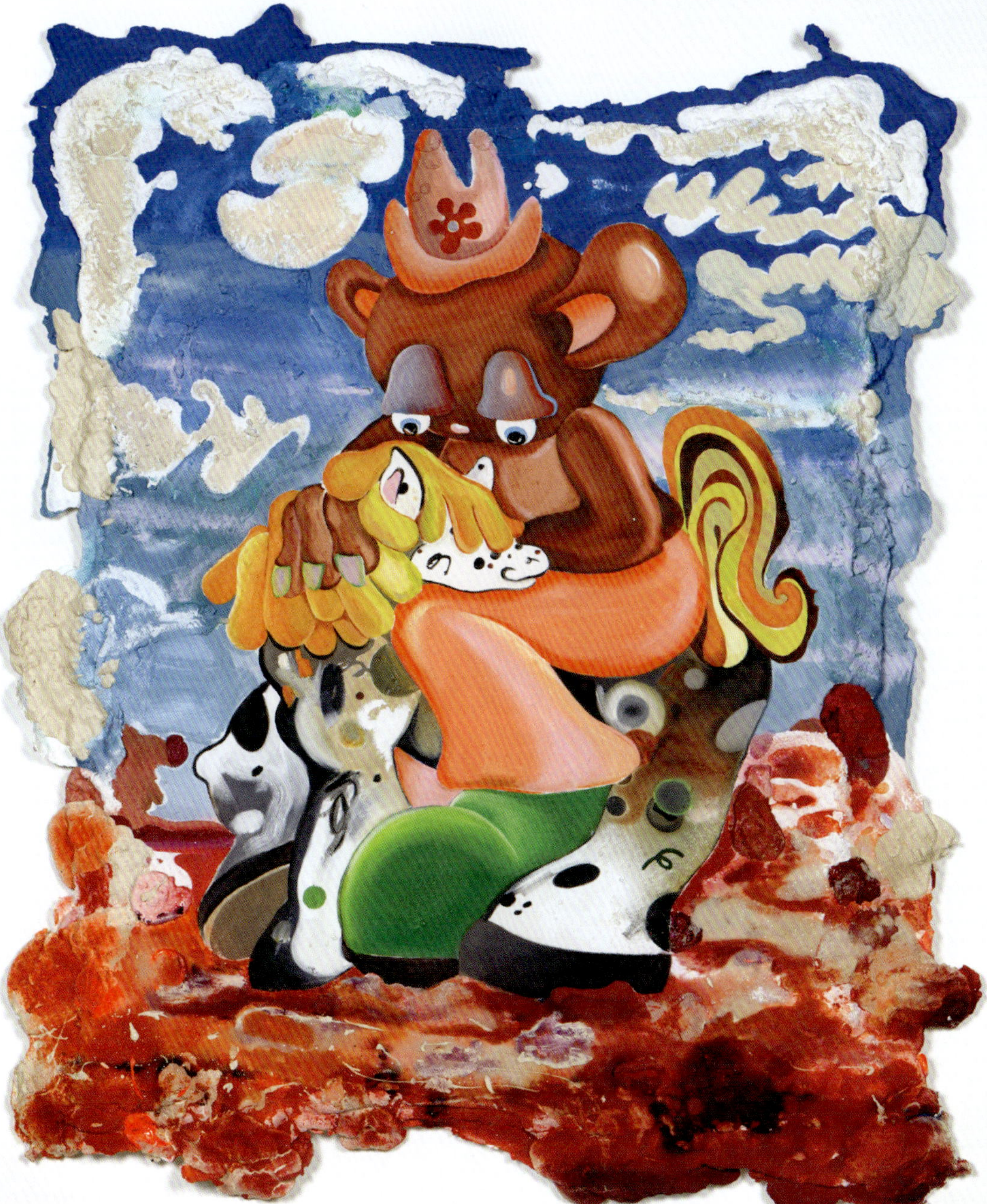

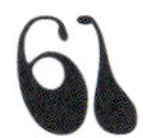

Big Brown Bear and Scribbles Trek
Through Red Rock Swamp, 2018

Oil, acrylic, Flashe, flour, and sand on canvas
44 × 34 inches

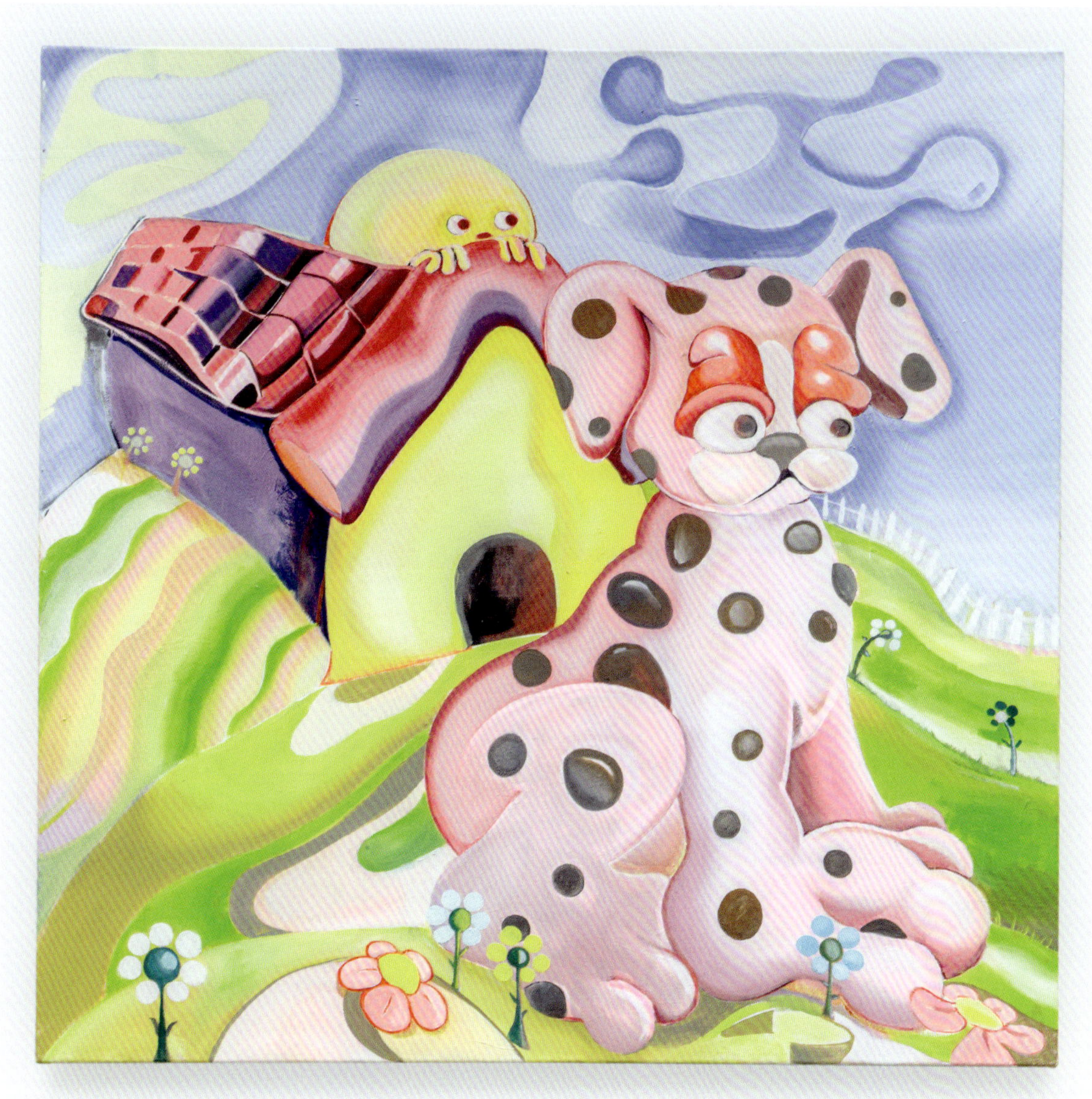

Spotty Dotty Dog House, 2020

Oil on canvas
36 × 36 inches

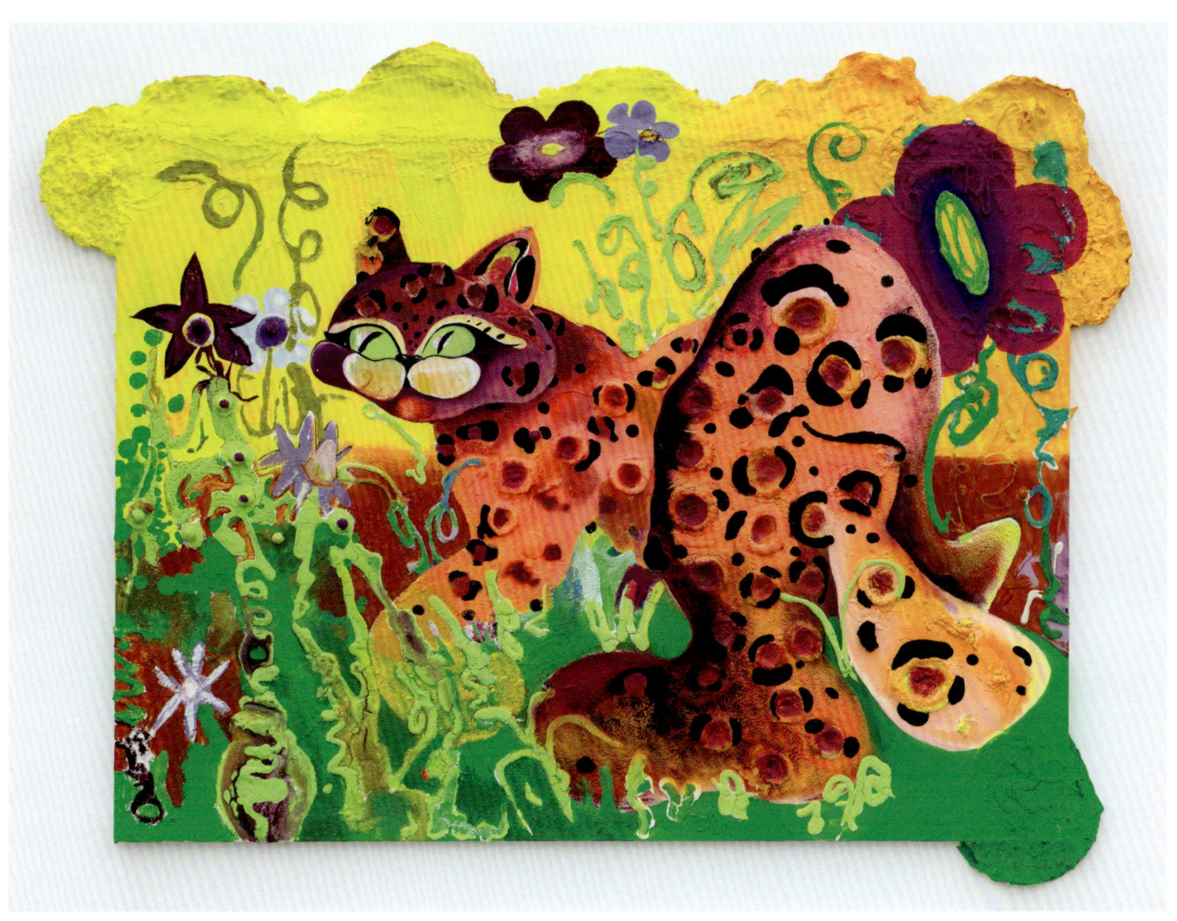

Cheetah, 2018

Oil, plaster, glue paper, and flour on canvas
40 × 50 inches

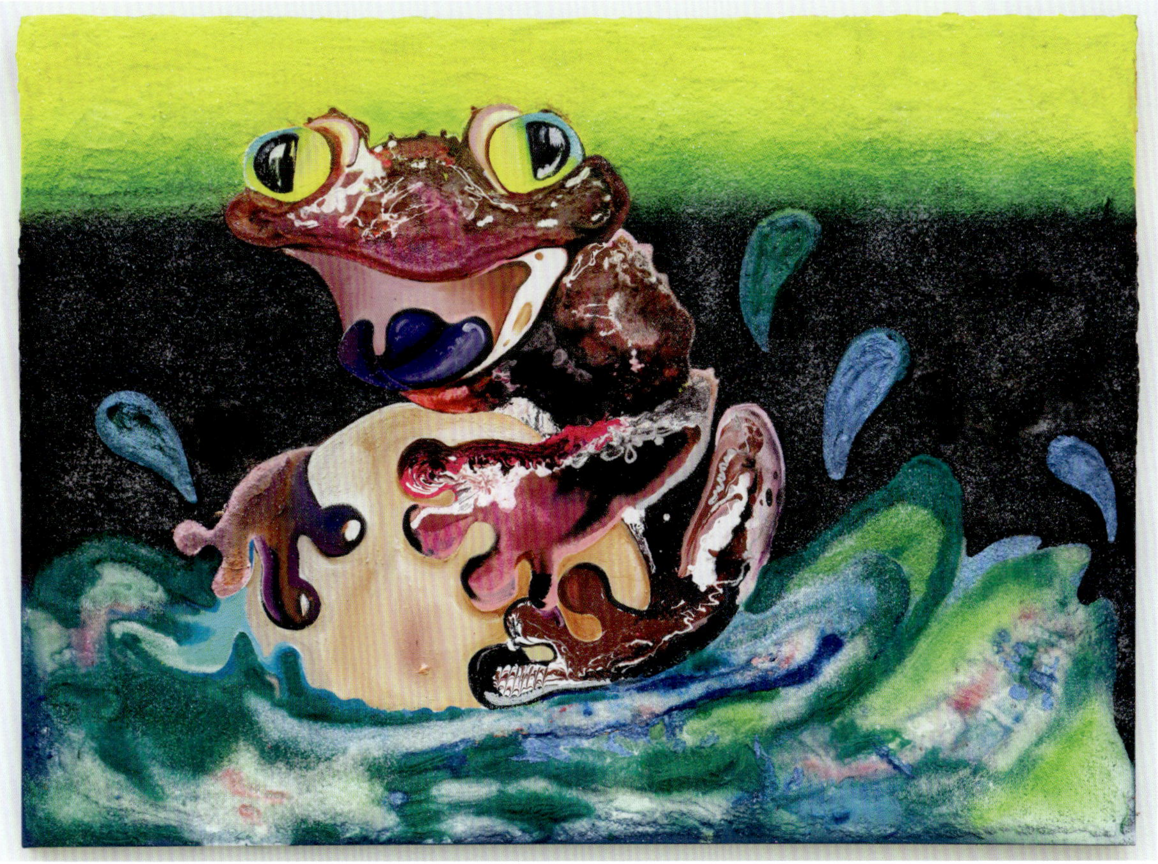

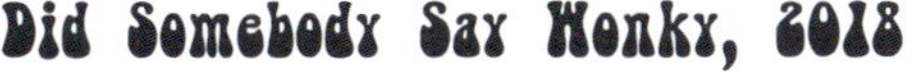

Did Somebody Say Wonky, 2018

Oil, acrylic, sand, and glitter on canvas
24 × 30 inches

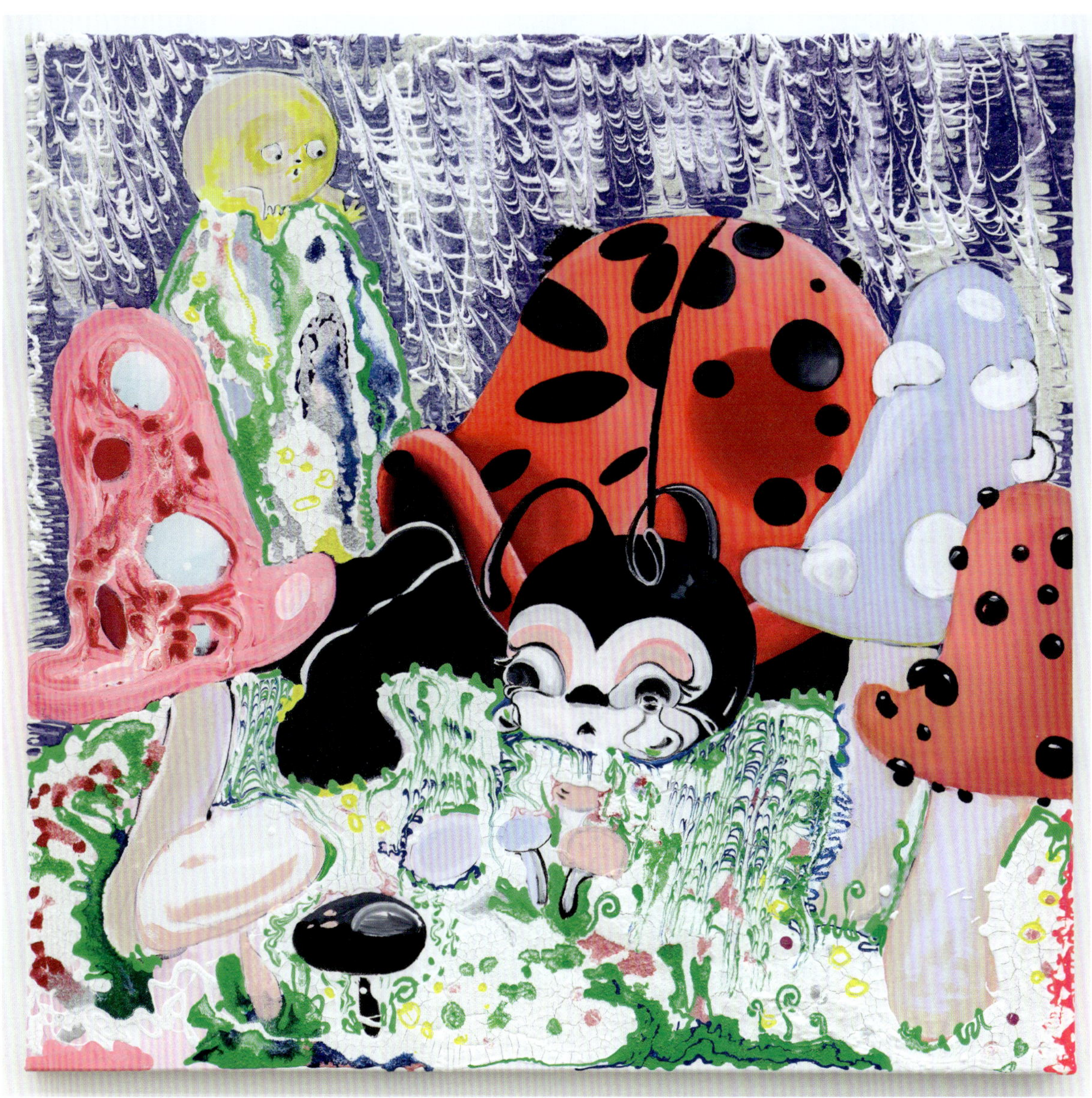

Ladybug, 2018

Oil, plaster, glue paper, and flour on canvas
40 × 40 inches

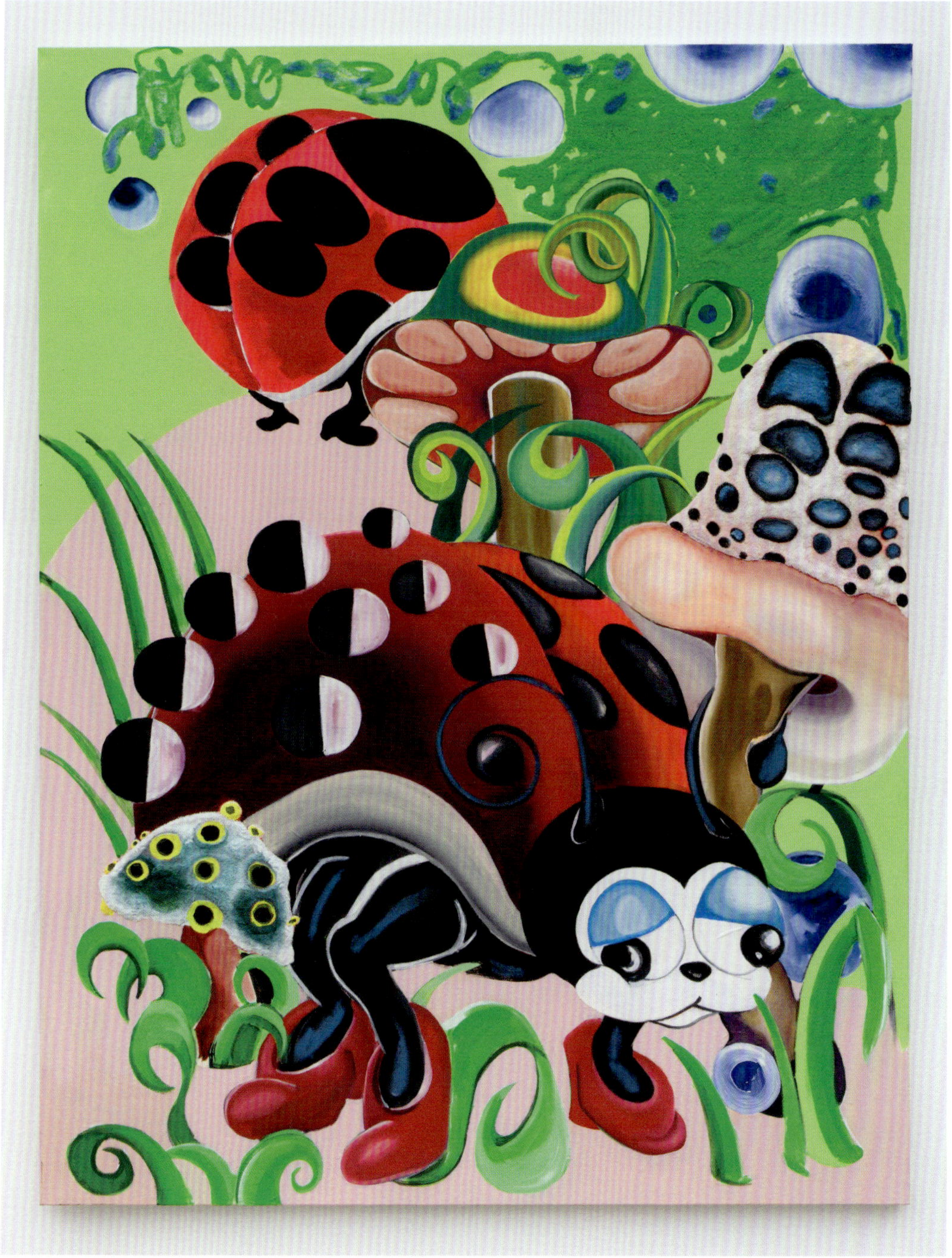

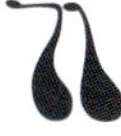

Untitled, 2019

Oil paint, Flashe vinyl paint, sand, and glitter on canvas
48 × 36 inches

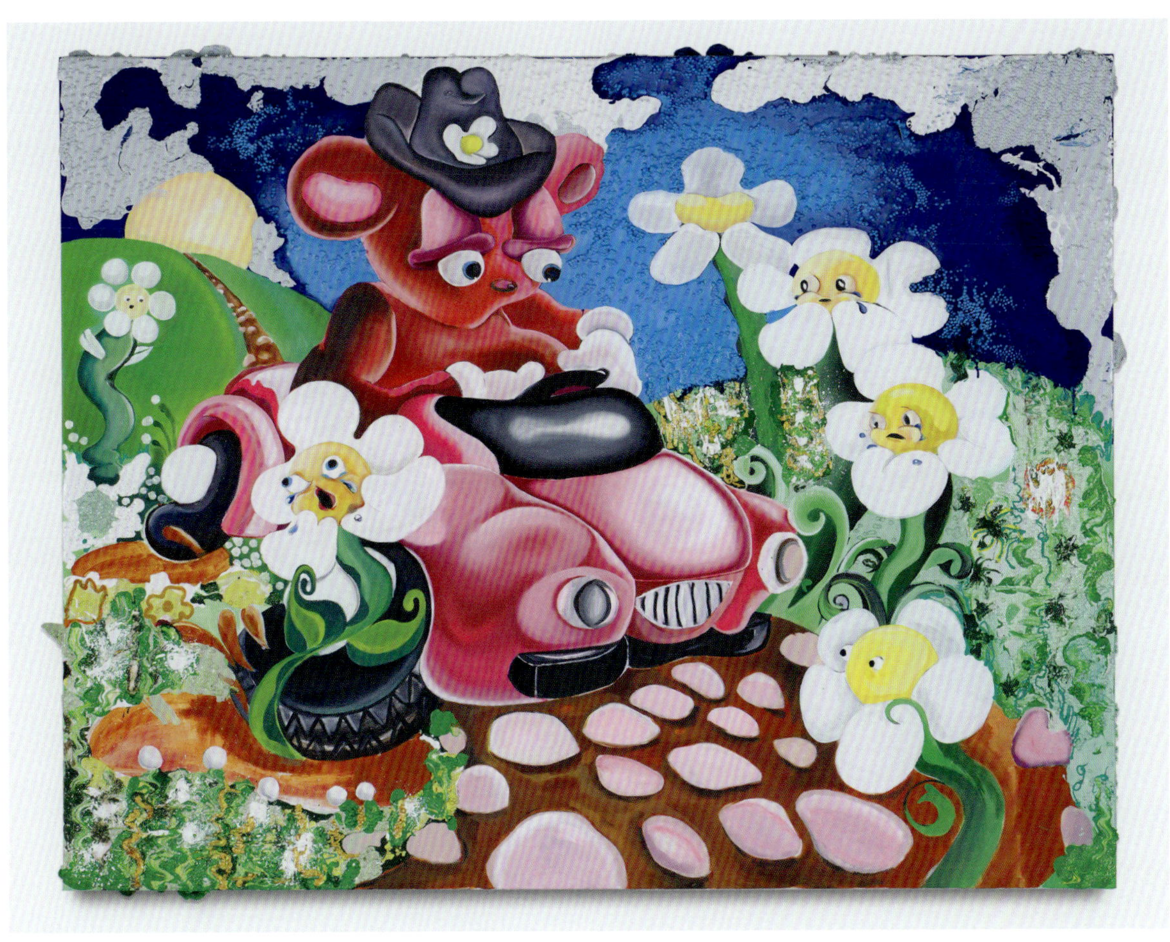

Buggy Bear is Out Of Control On The Long and Winding Road, 2019

Oil, Flashe, acrylic, styrofoam, glitter
50 × 60 inches

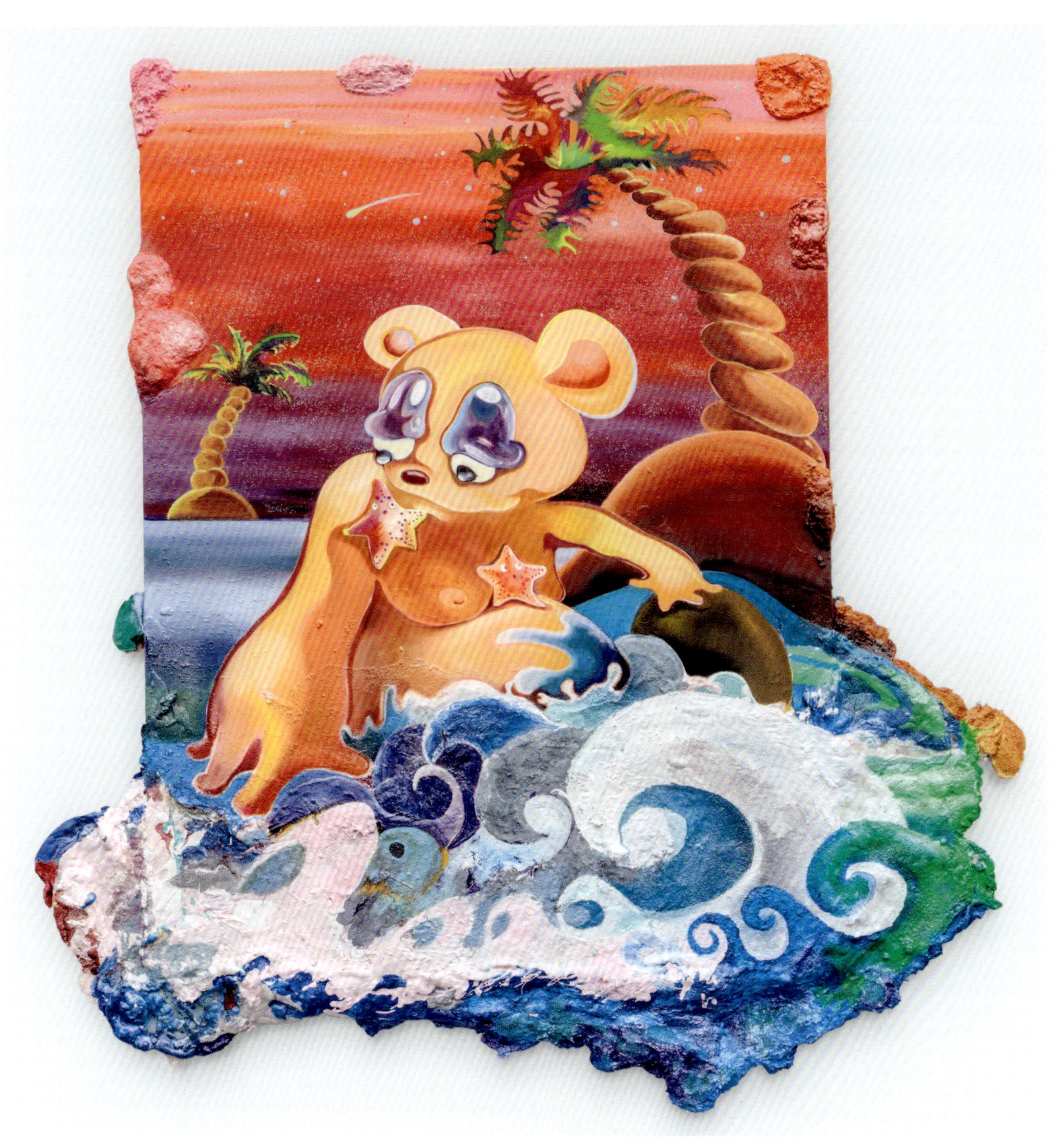

Wet N' Wild, 2020

Oil, Flashe, glitter, clay on canvas
45 × 36 inches

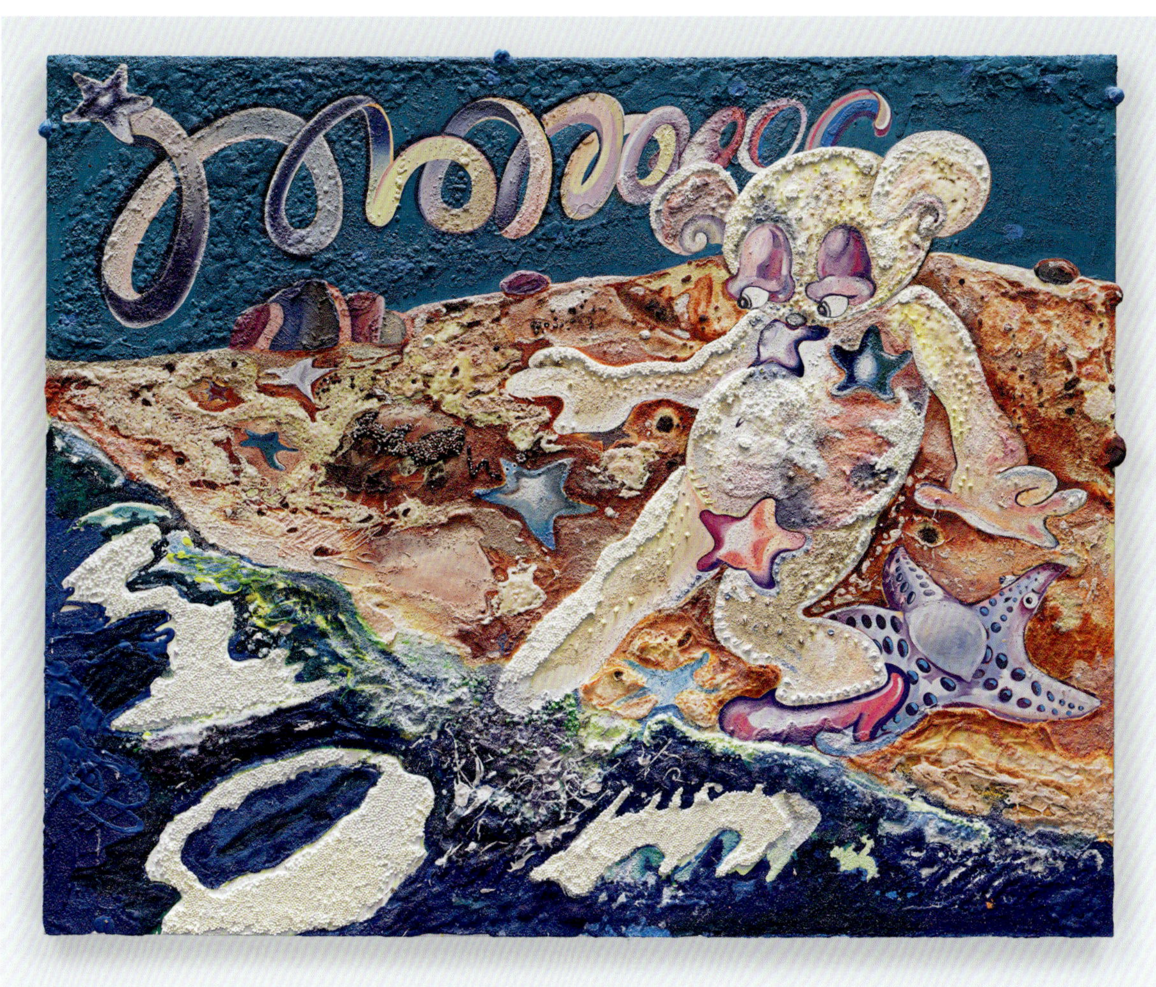

**Buggy Bear on a Star Studded
Beach Adventure, 2021**

Oil paint, glitter, sand, styrofoam balls, and salt on canvas
60 × 72 × 2 ½ inches

77

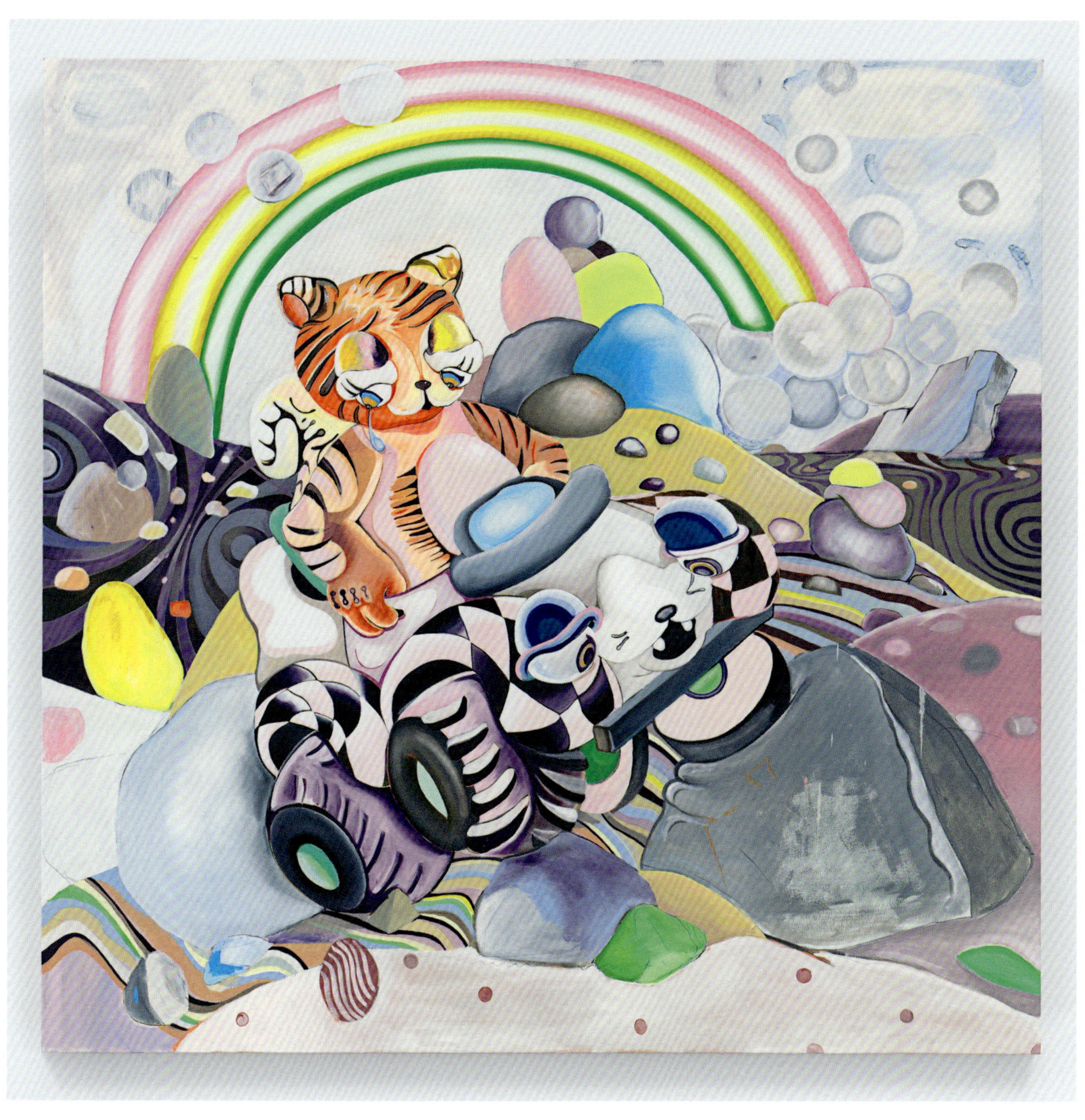

Tippy Tiger Between a Rock and a Boulder, 2021

Oil paint and glitter on canvas
60 × 60 × 1 ½ inches

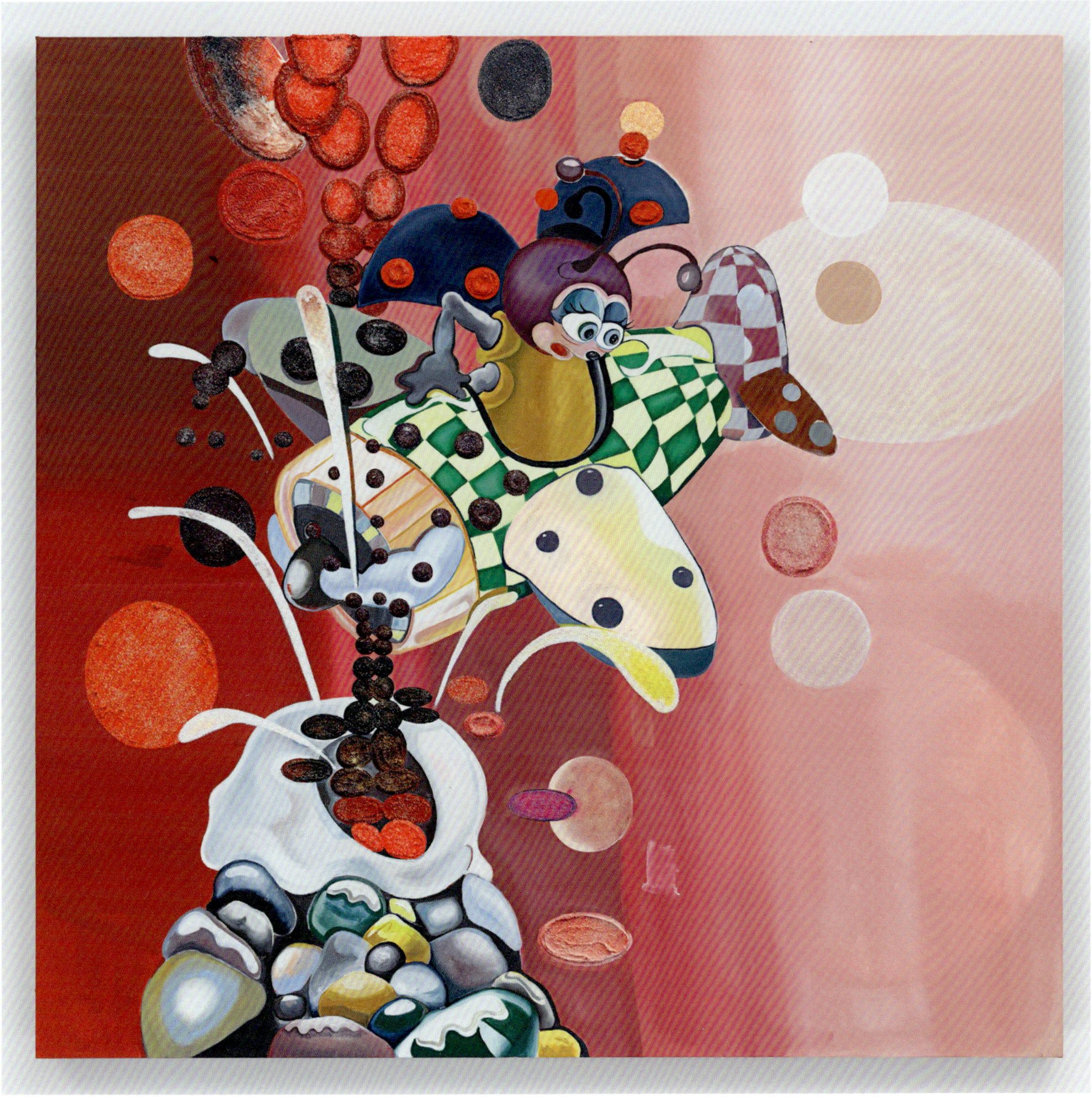

Lady Opposite Dots is Losing Her Spots, 2021

Oil paint, glitter, Flashe, and puff additive on canvas
60 × 60 × 1 ½ inches

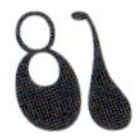

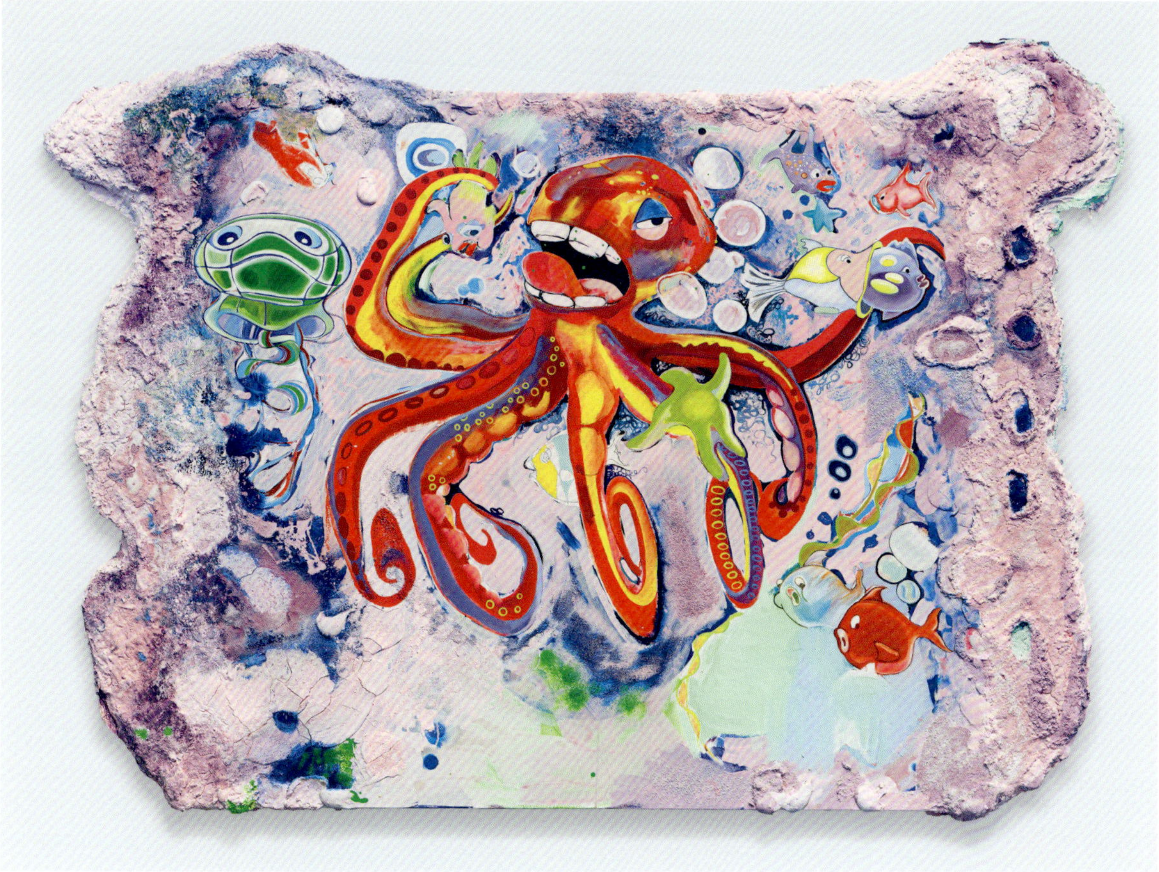

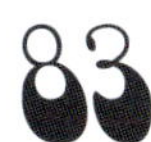

Tell Me Another Joke, 2021

Acrylic paint, sand, flour, glitter, oil paint,
and papier-mâché on canvas
64 × 92 × 2 ½ inches

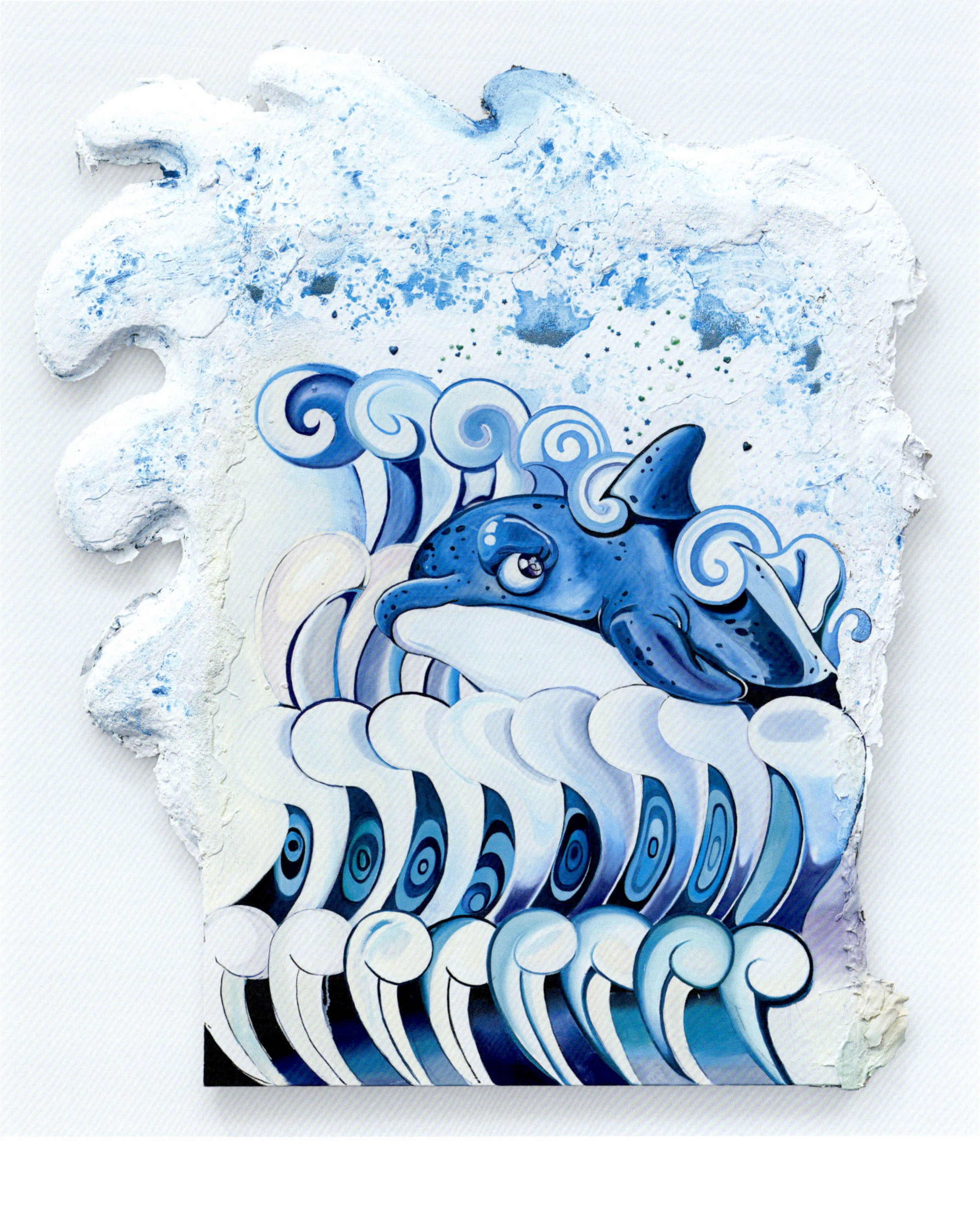

Major Wave, 2021

Acrylic paint, gel polish, sand, flour, glitter,
oil paint, and papier-mâché on canvas
59 × 48 × 2 ½ inches

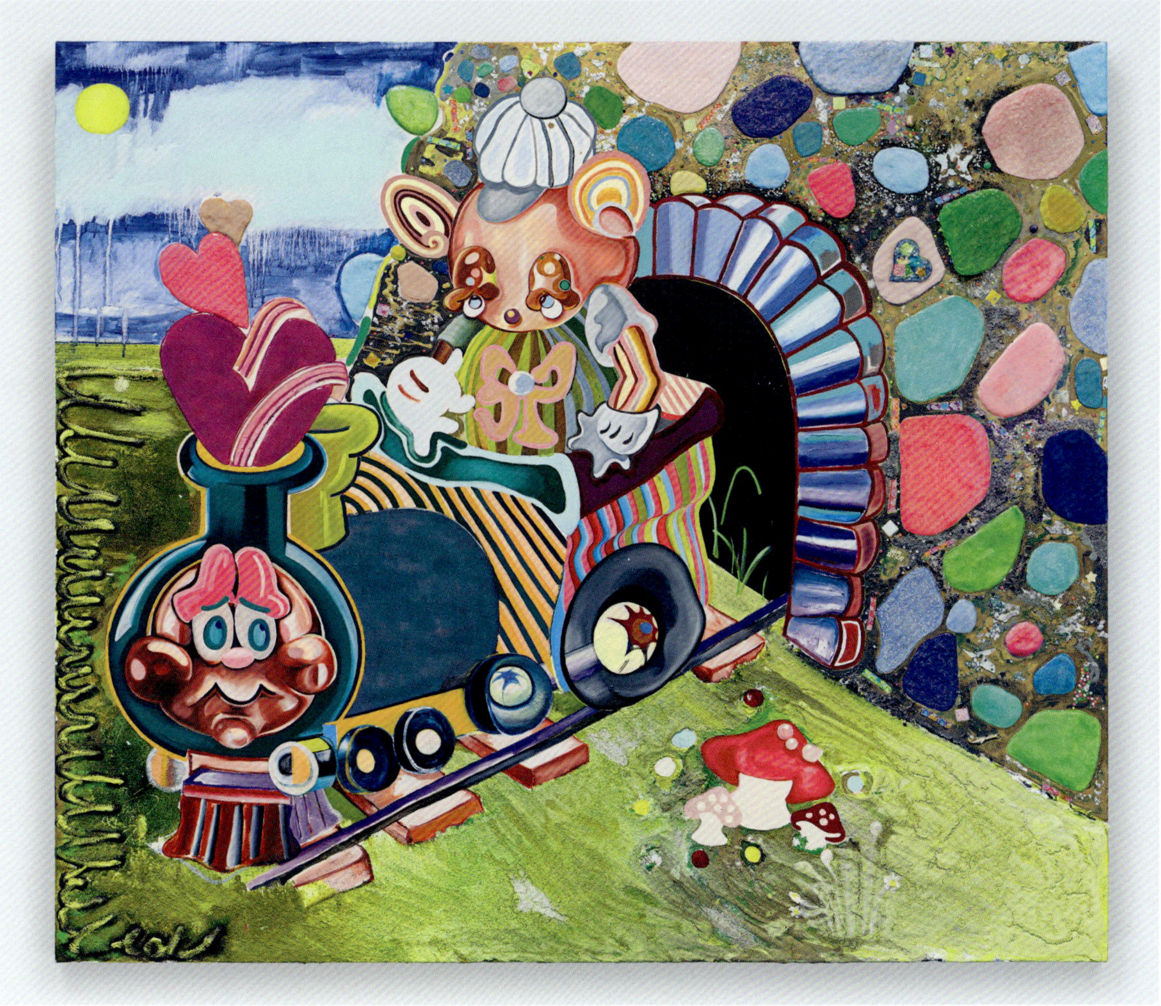

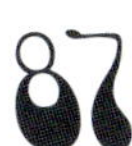

Oil, Flashe, glitter, polygel, confetti, rhinestones, and acrylic sculpting powder on canvas
60 × 68 × 1 ½ inches

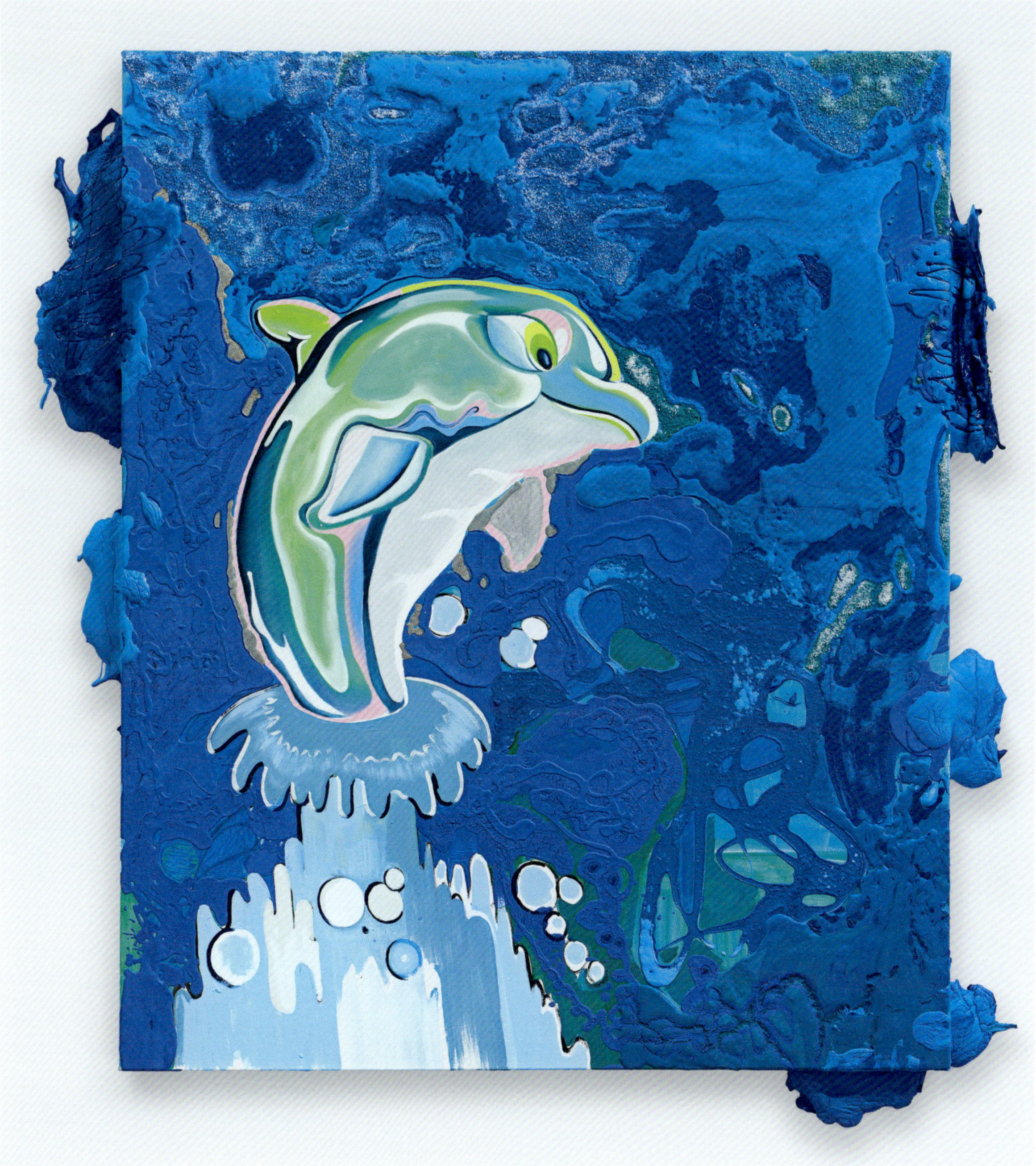

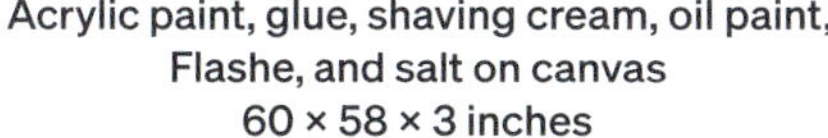

Splash, 2021

Acrylic paint, glue, shaving cream, oil paint,
Flashe, and salt on canvas
60 × 58 × 3 inches

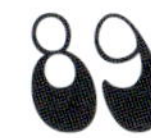

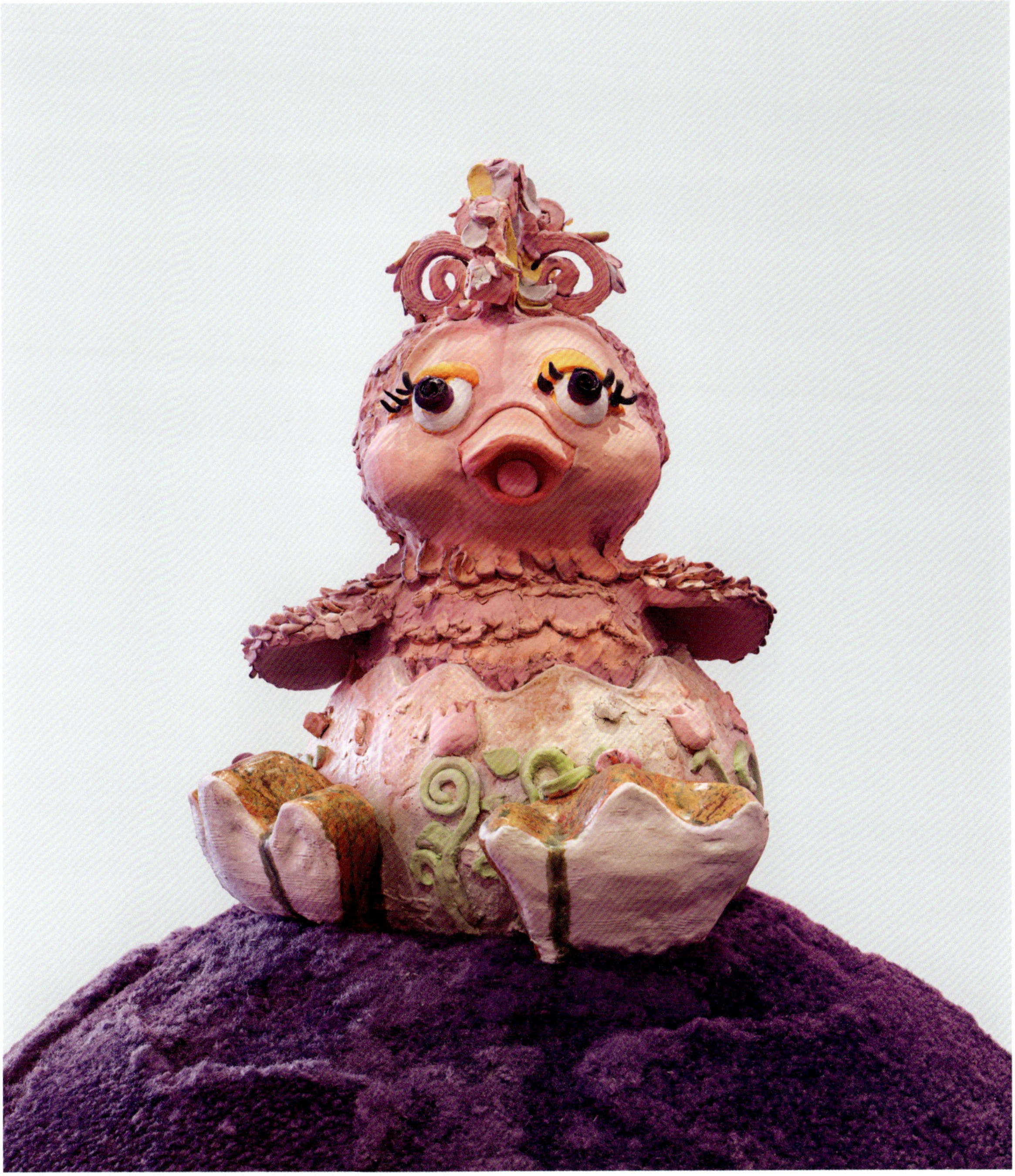

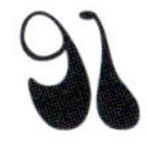

Baby Chick, 2021

Glazed ceramic and Flashe
18 × 13 × 13 inches

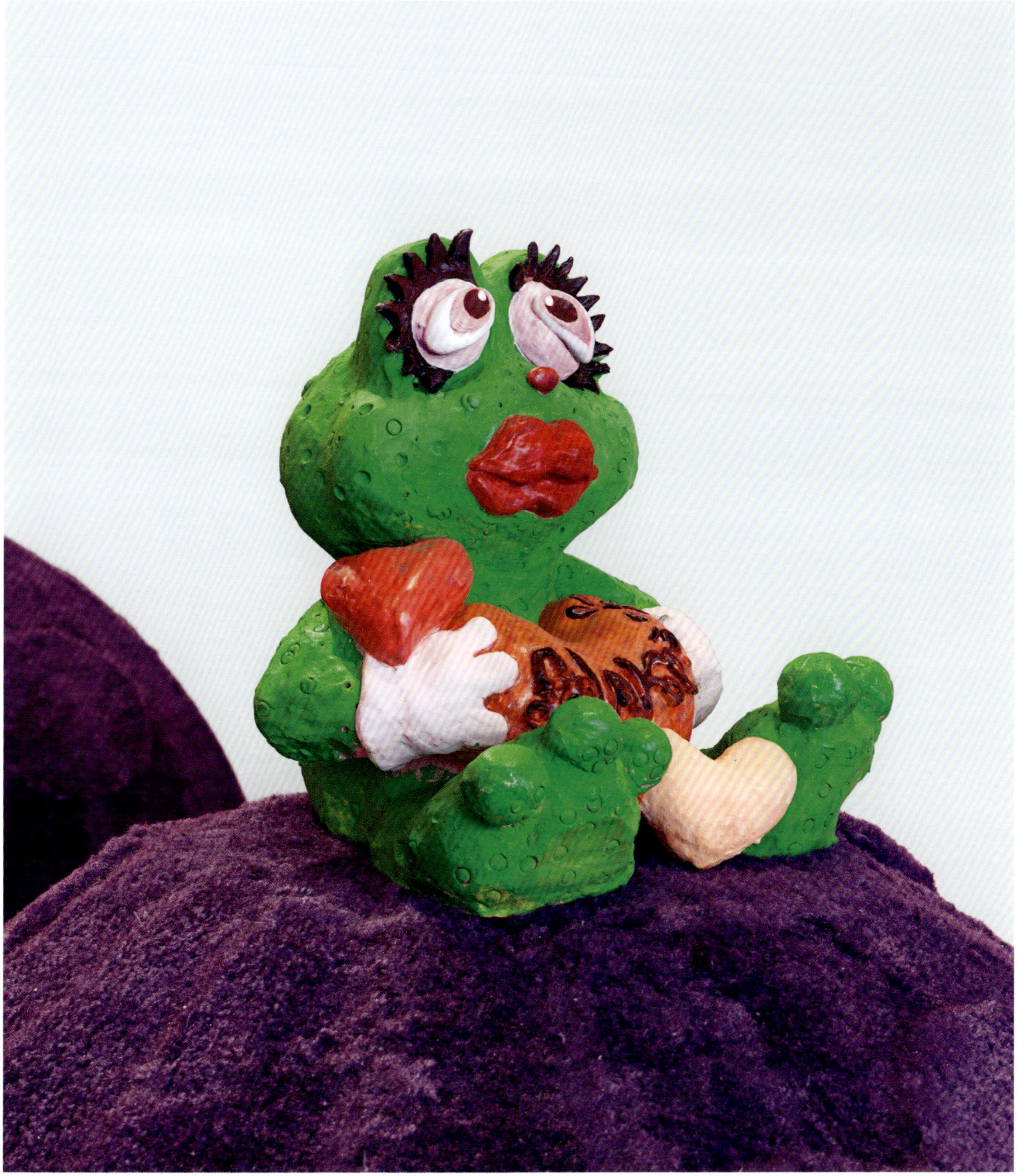

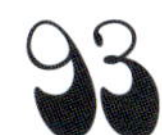

Little Frog Loves Alake, 2021
Glazed ceramic and enamel paint
12 × 12 × 12 ½ inches

93

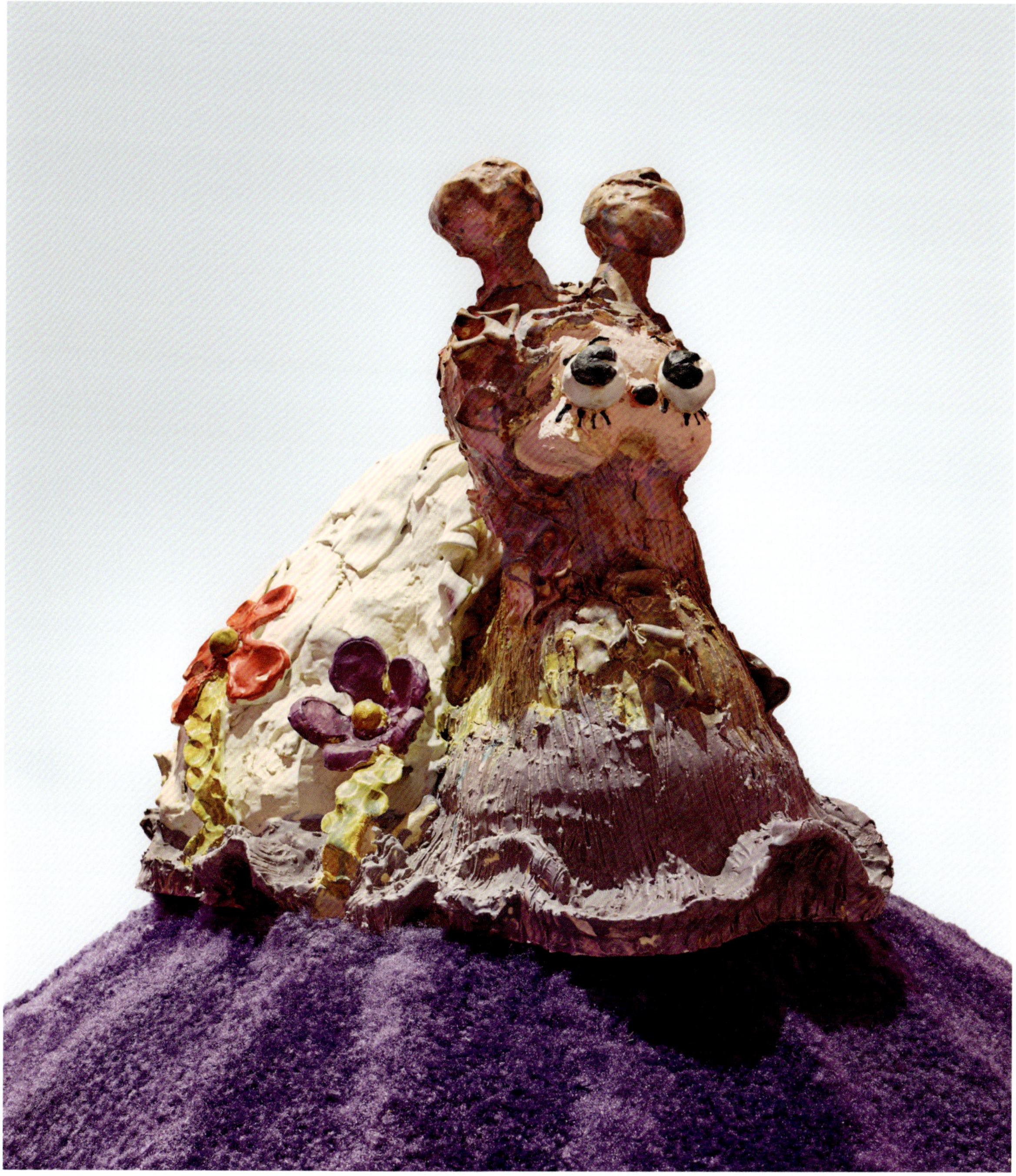

Snaily Boop, 2021

Glazed ceramic
15 × 13 × 18 ½ inches

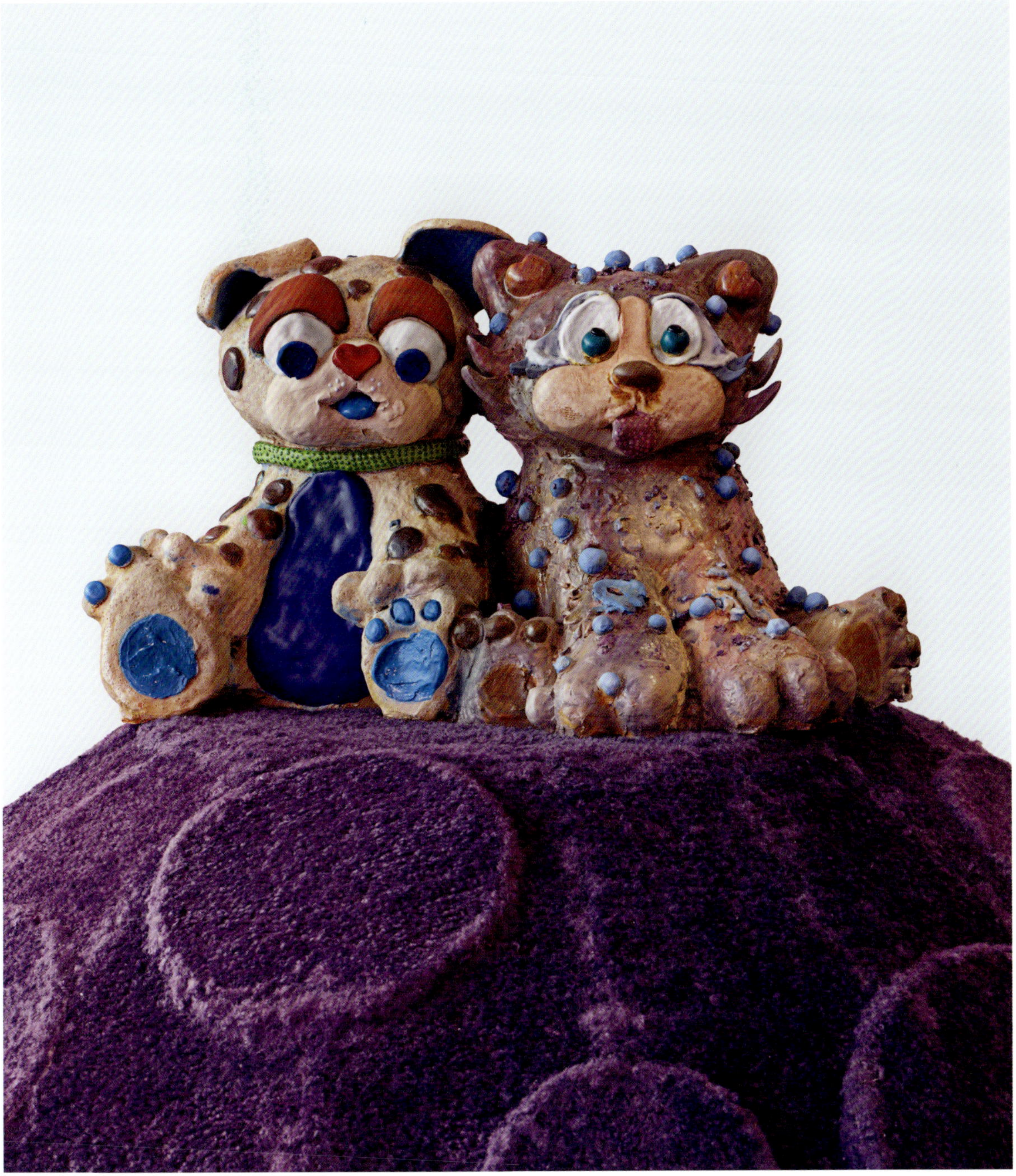

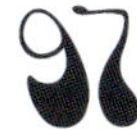

Best Buddies, 2021

Glazed ceramic and enamel paint
14 × 25 × 16 inches

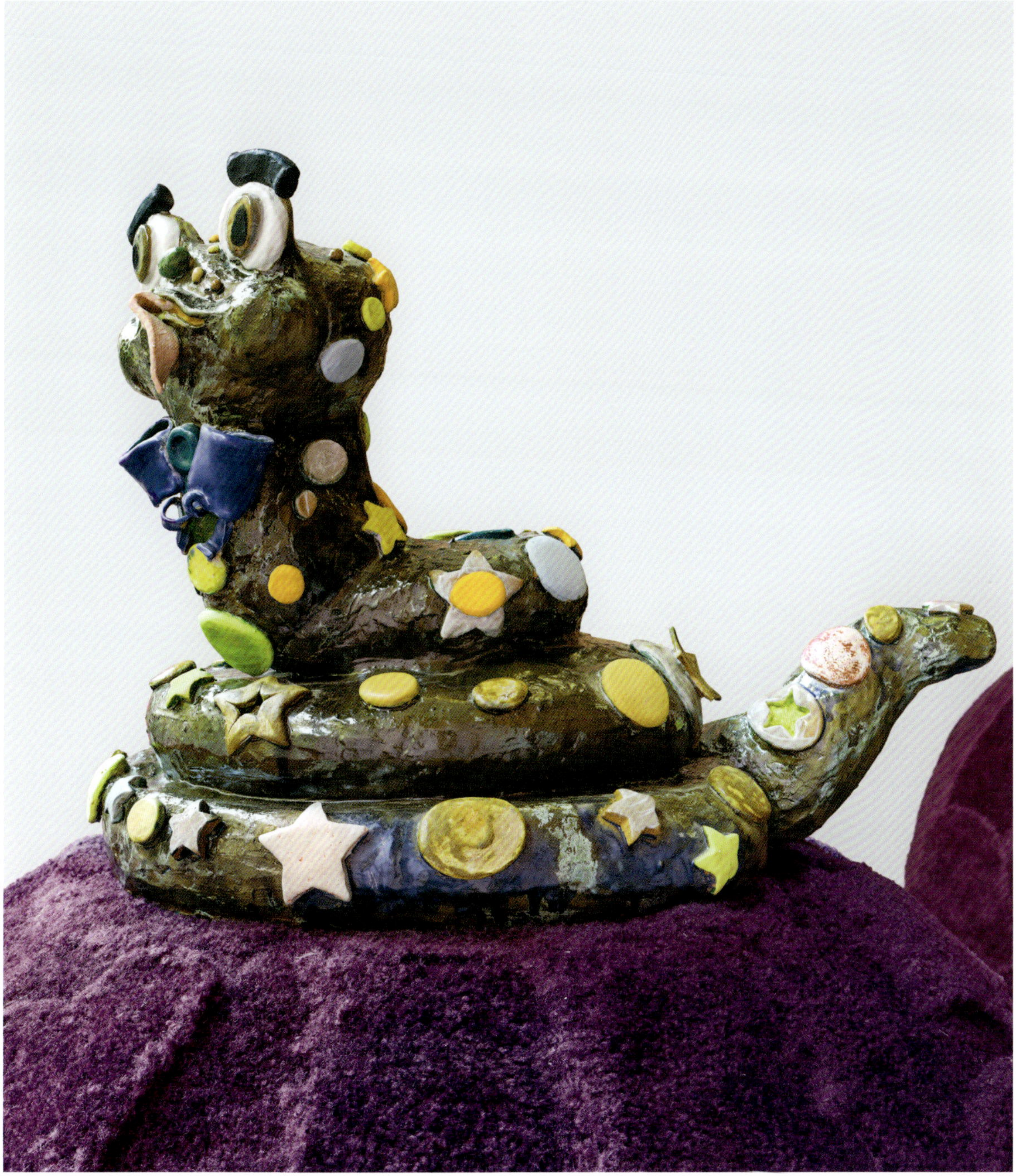

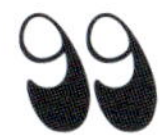

Mister Spitz, 2021
Glazed ceramic and enamel paint
18 × 24 × 25 inches

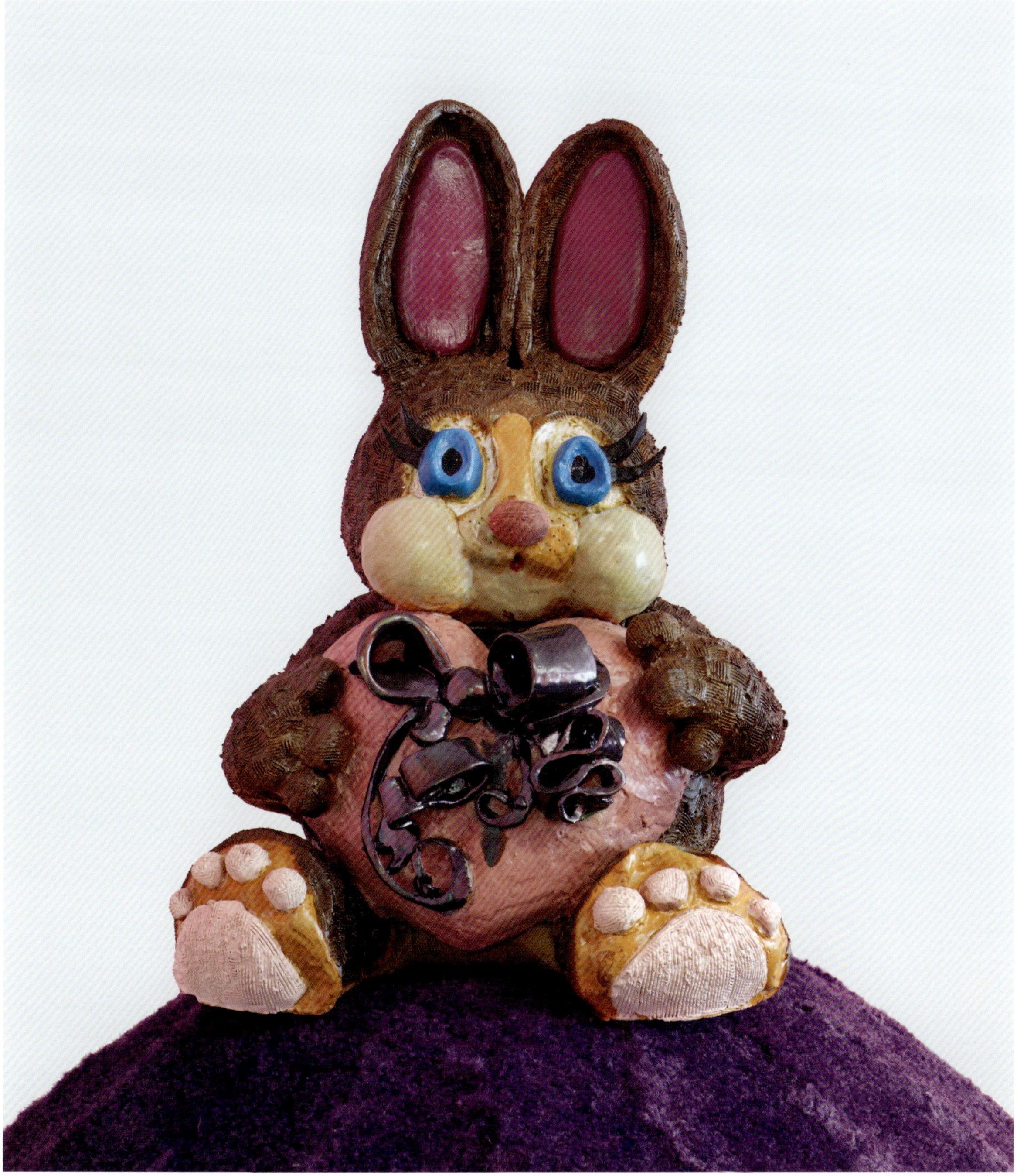

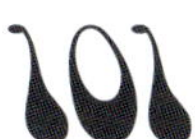

Chocolate Bunny Loves Everyone, 2021

Glazed ceramic
22 ½ x 15 × 15 inches

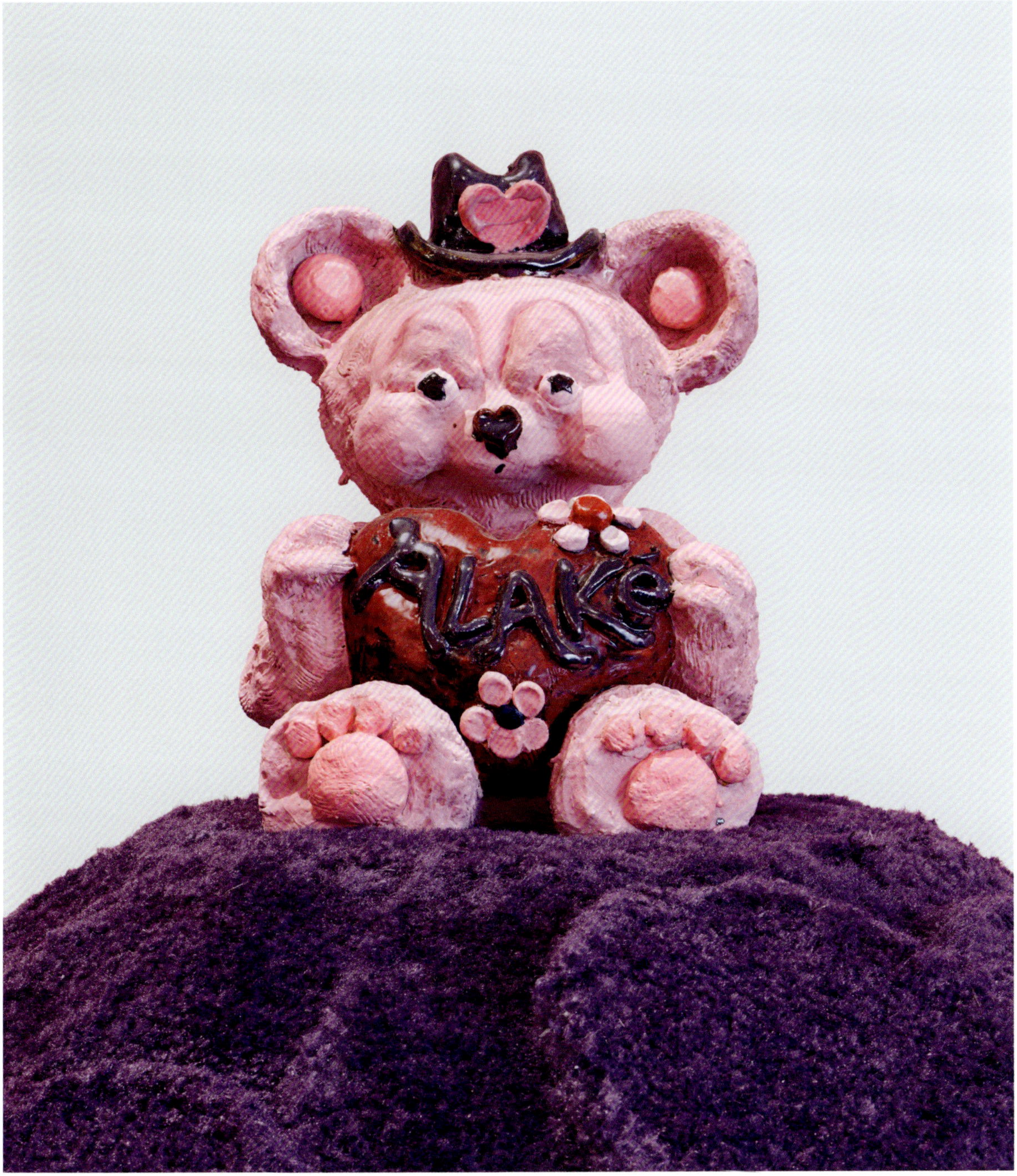

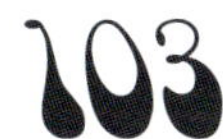

Baby Bear Loves Alake, 2021

Glazed ceramic and enamel paint
11 ½ x 8 × 9 inches

103

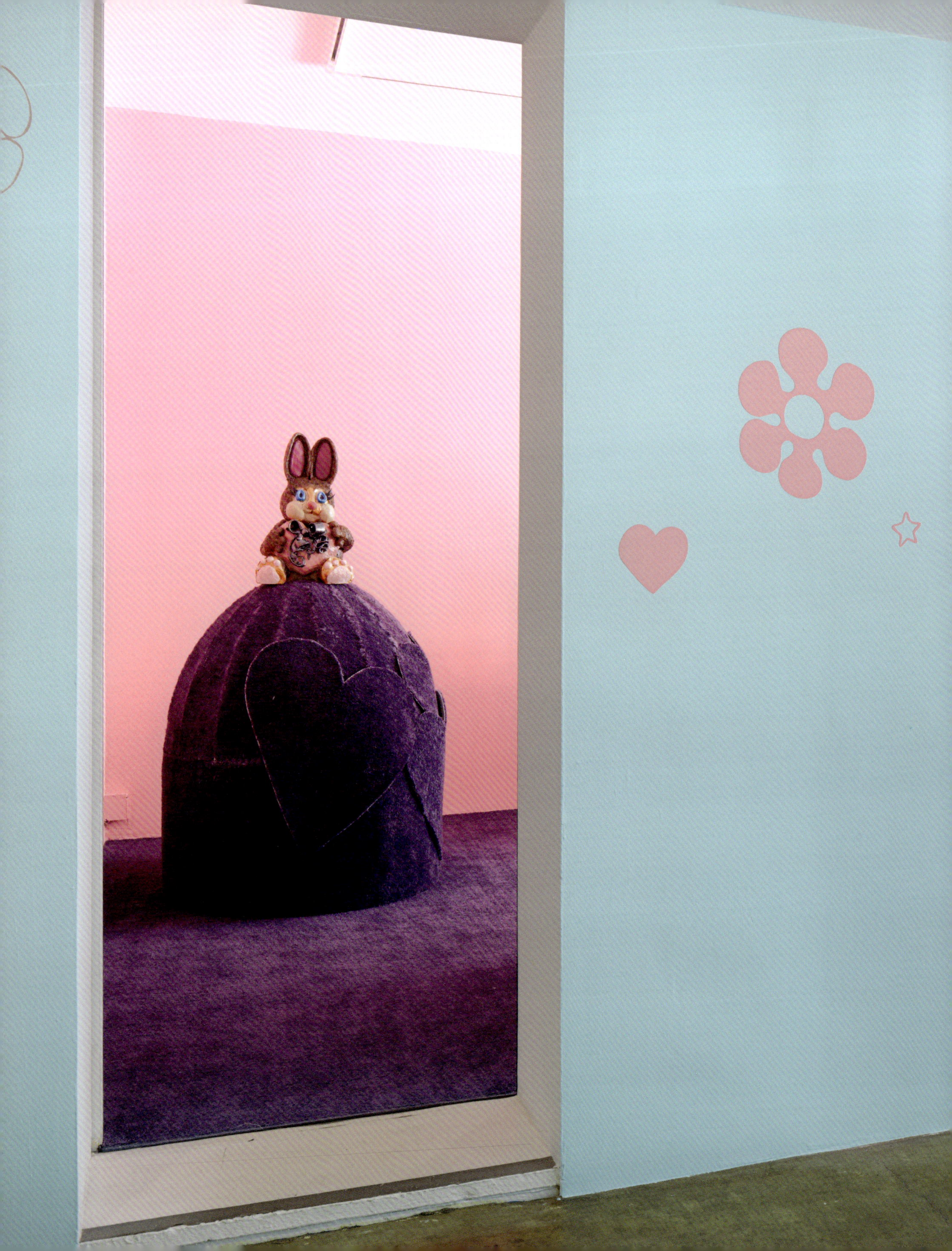

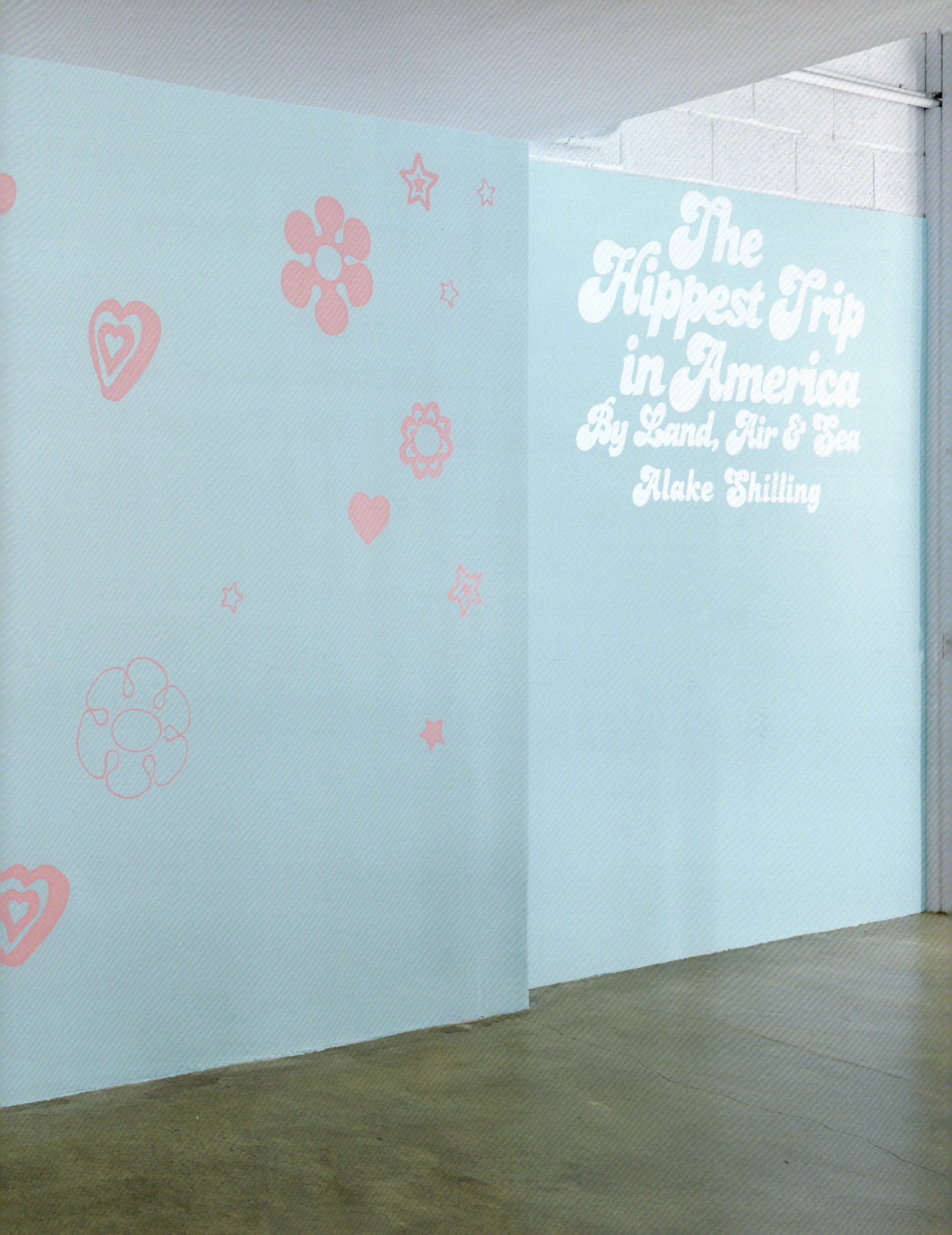

The Hippest Trip
in America
By Land, Air & Sea
Alake Shilling

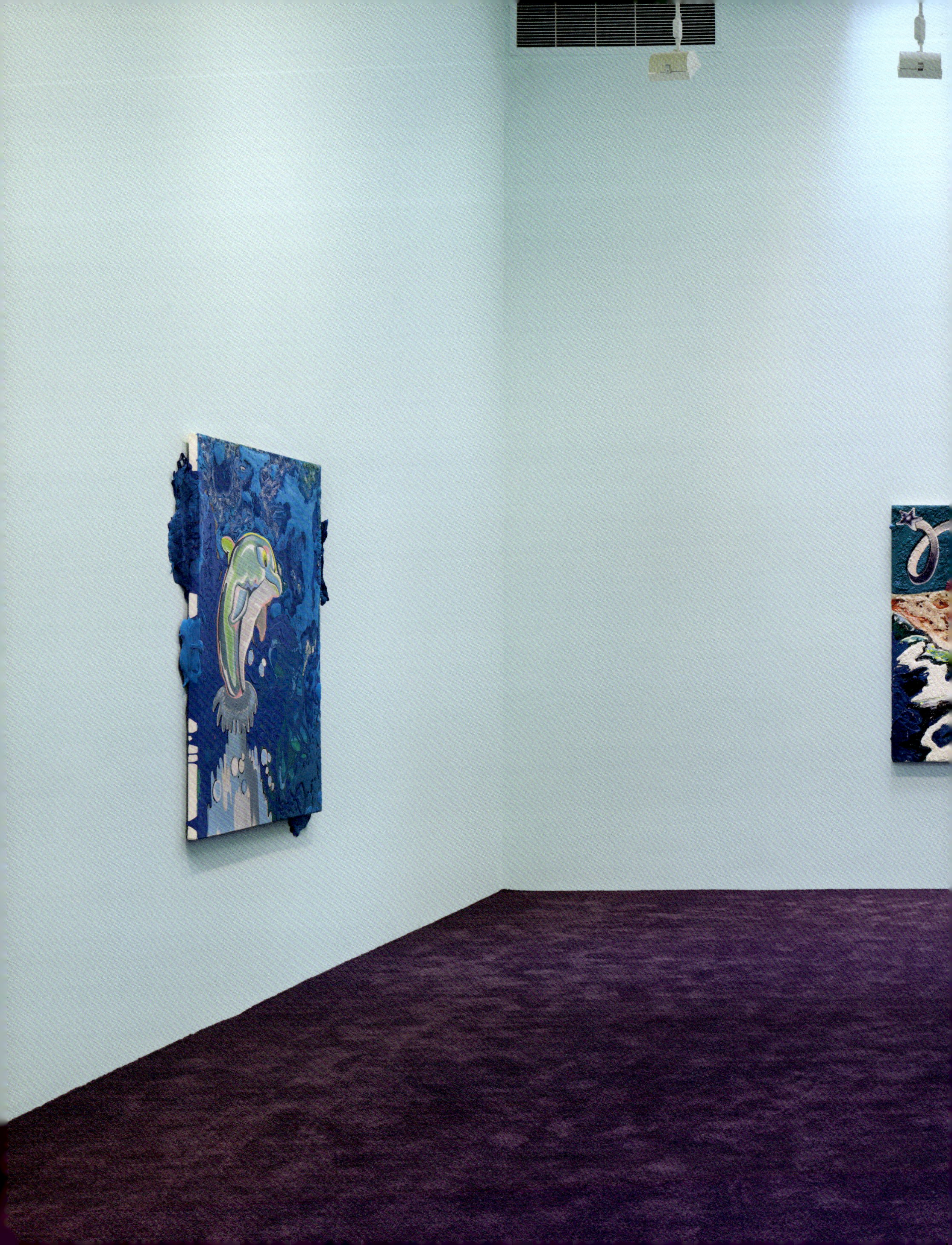

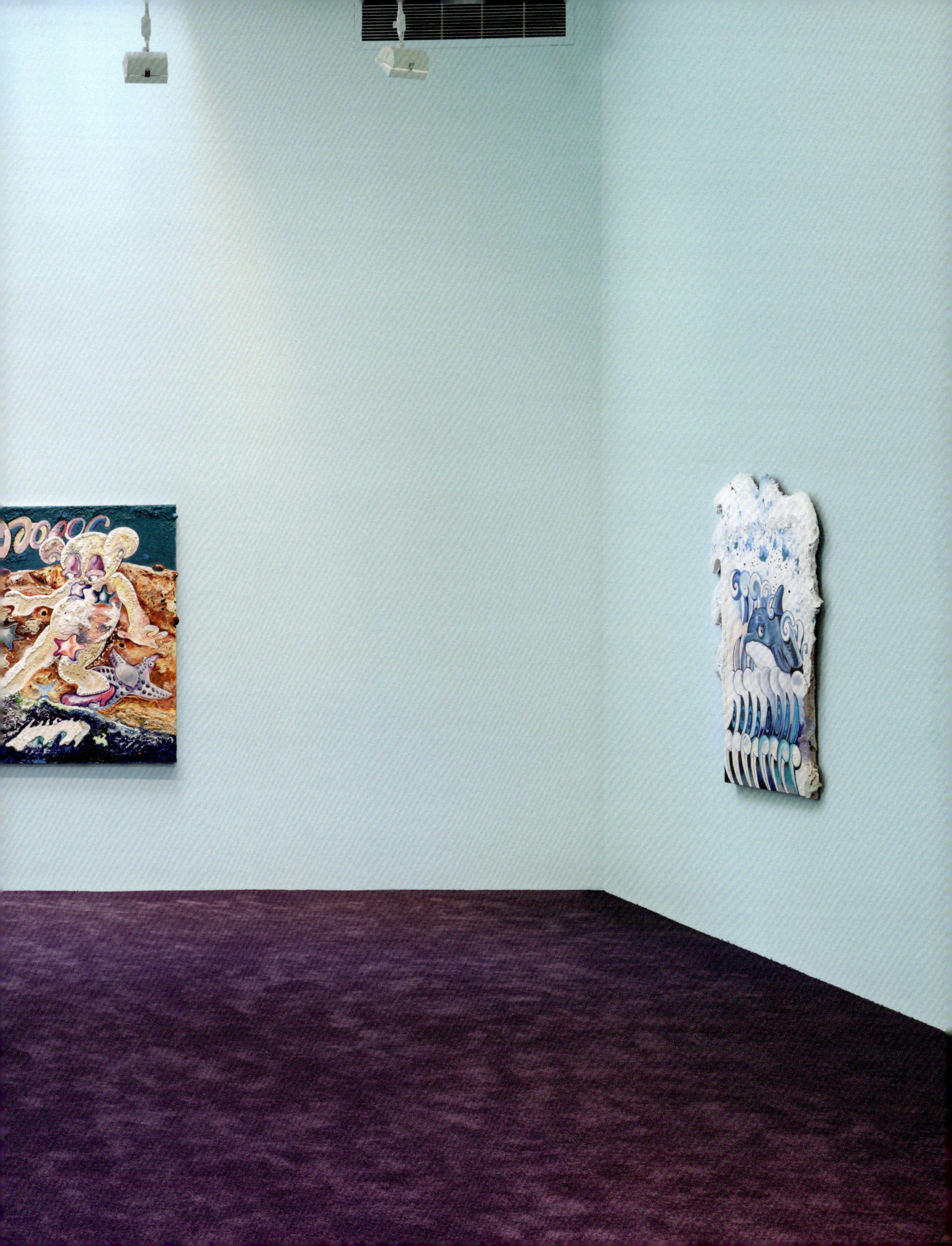

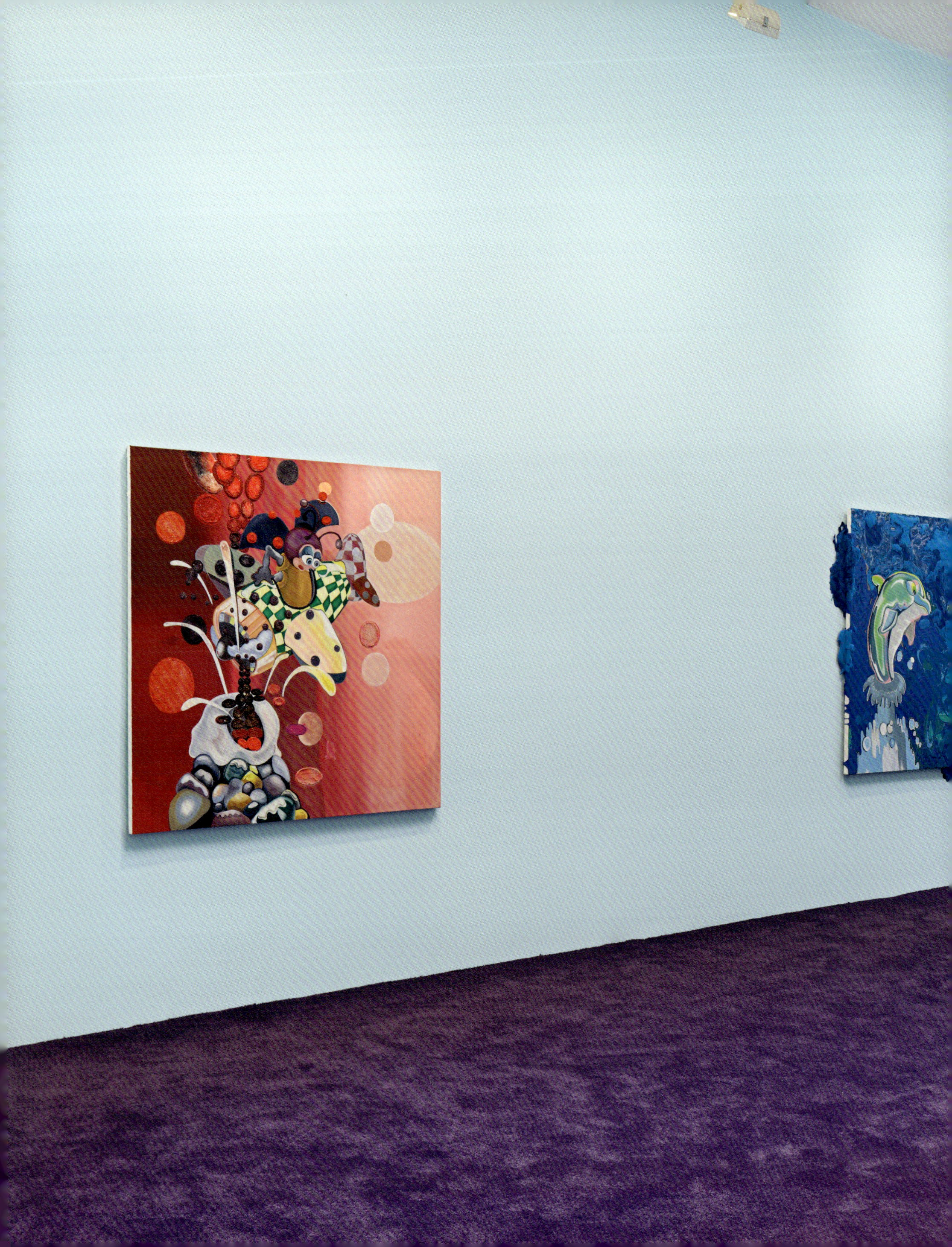

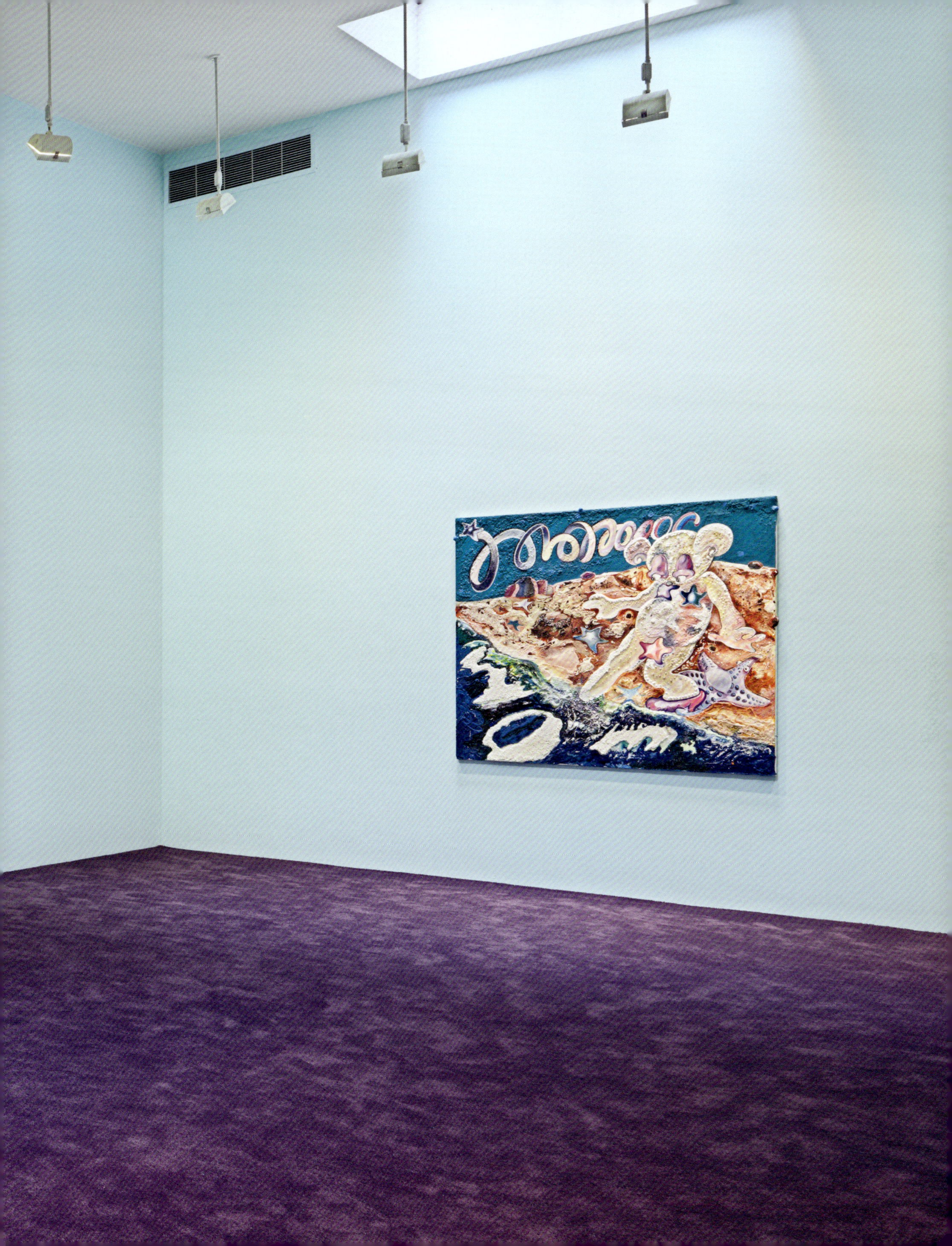

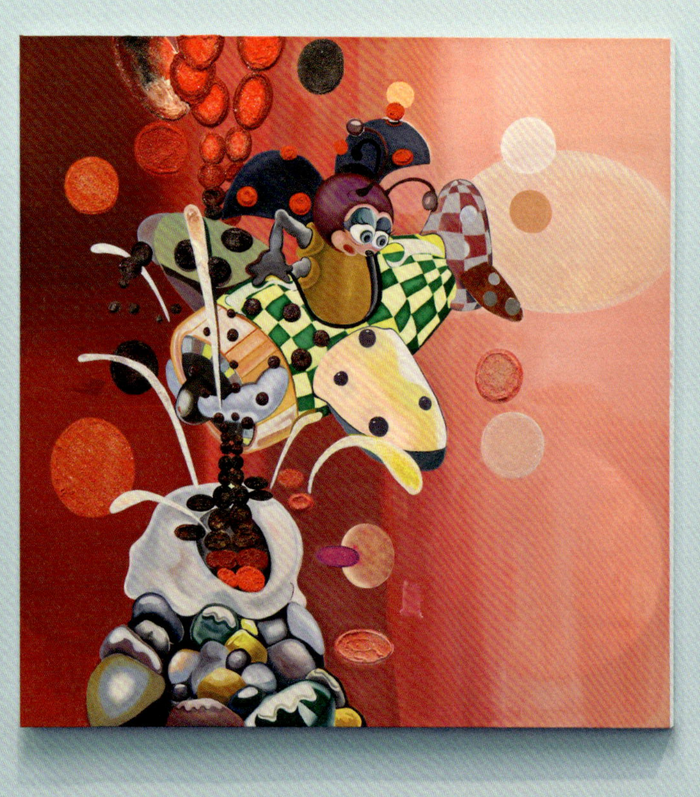

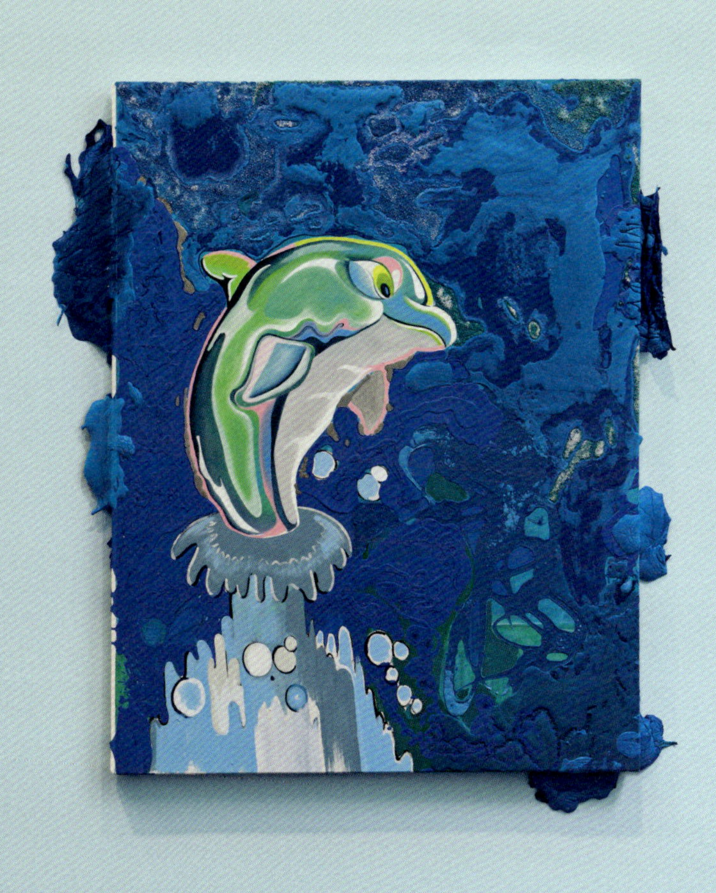

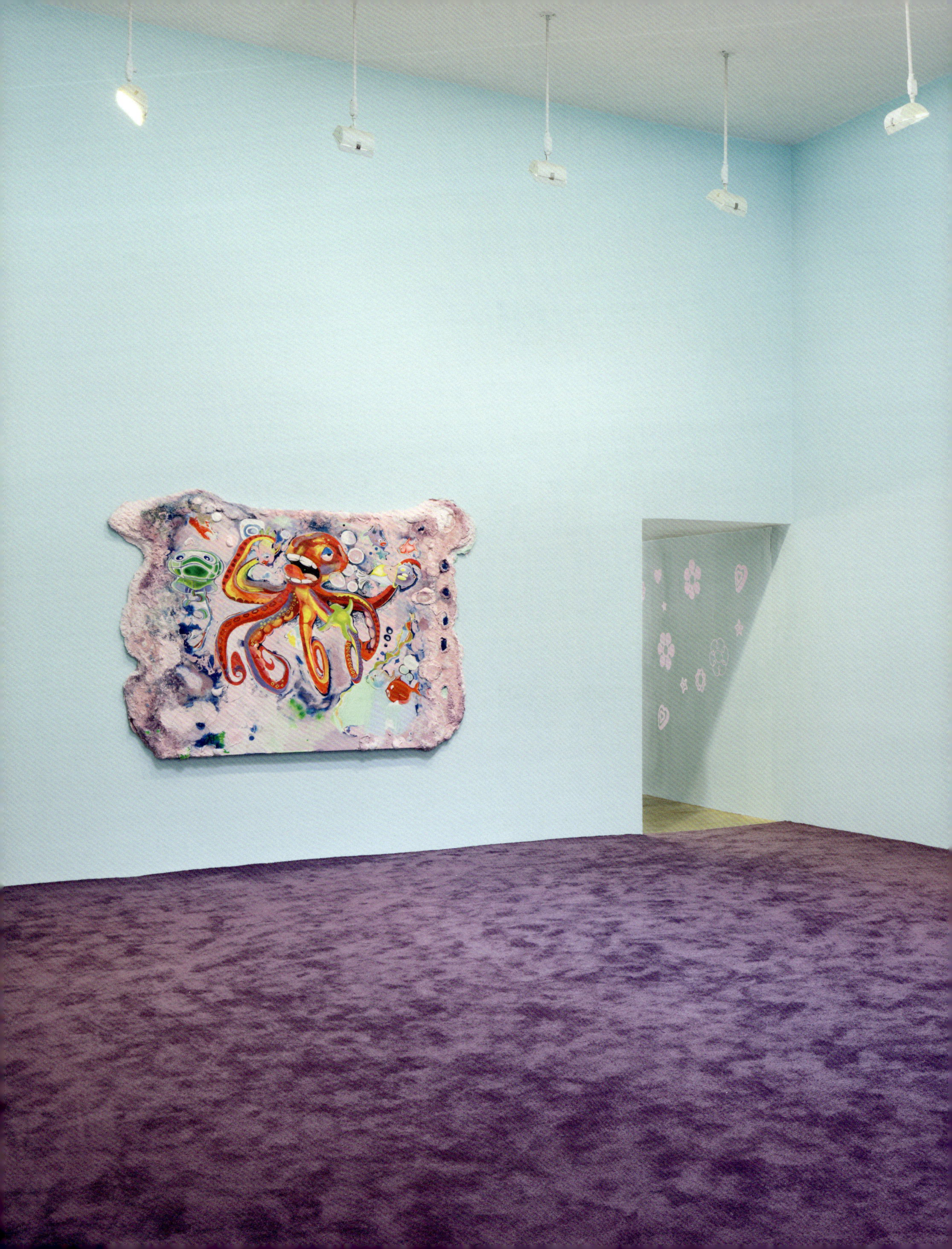

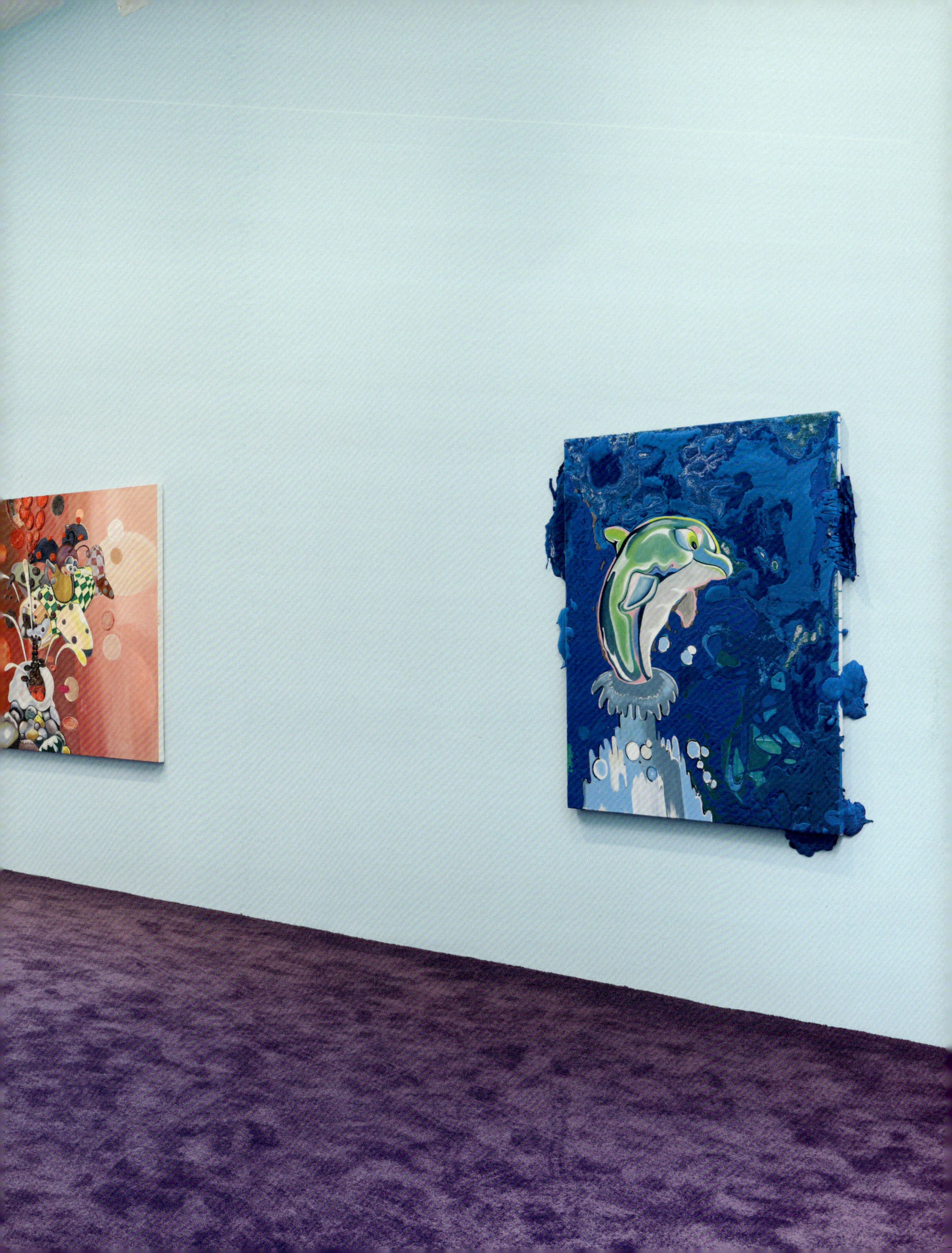

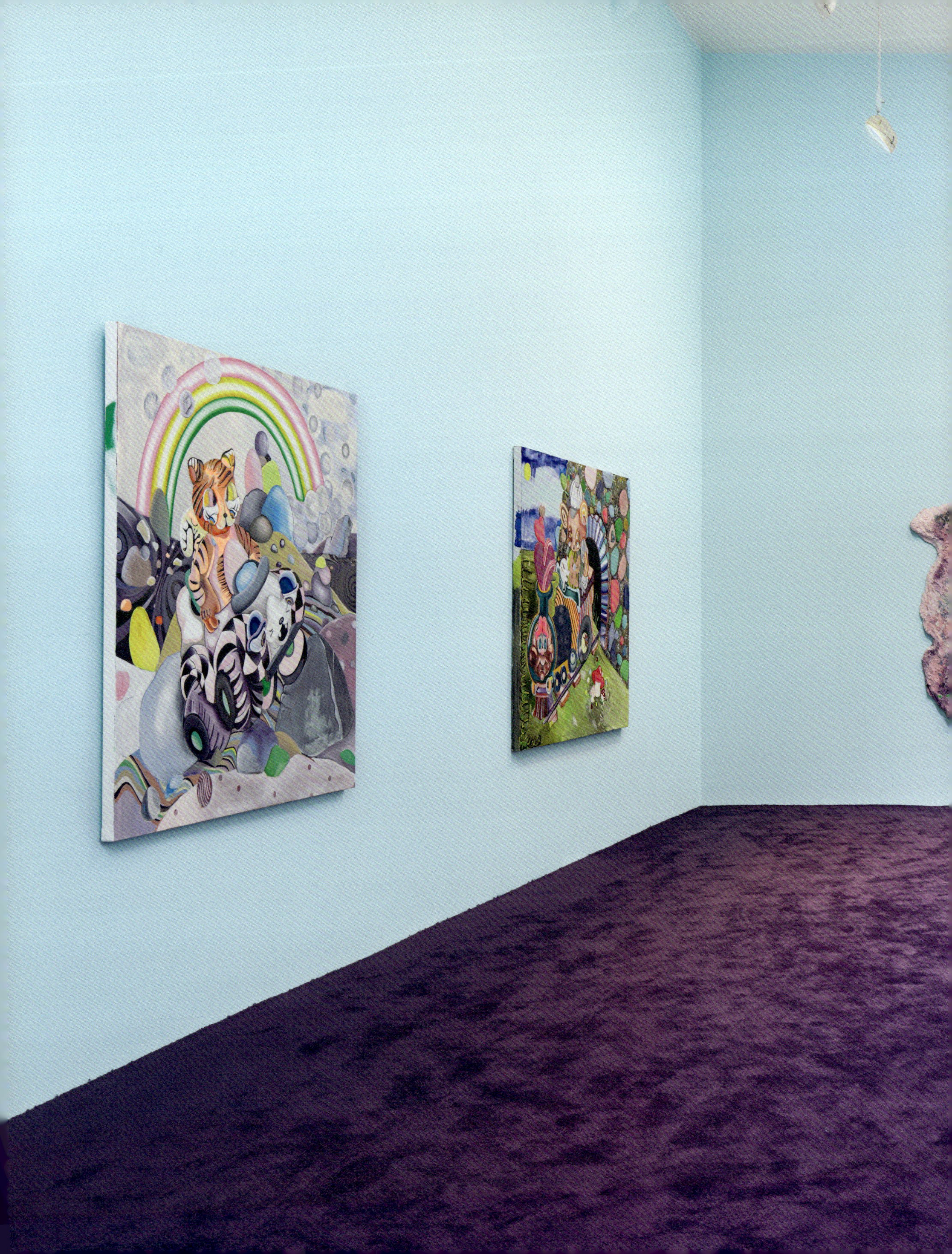

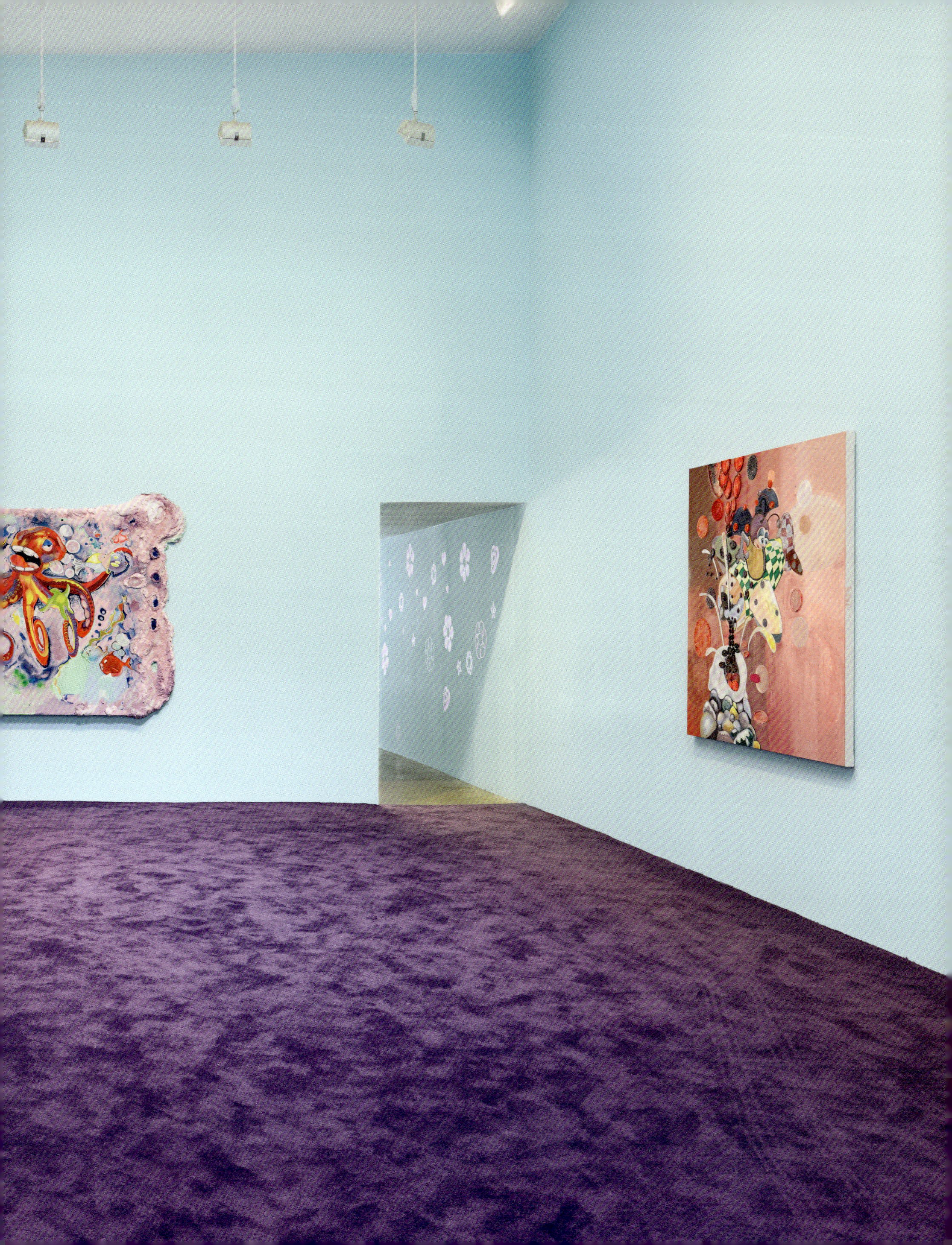

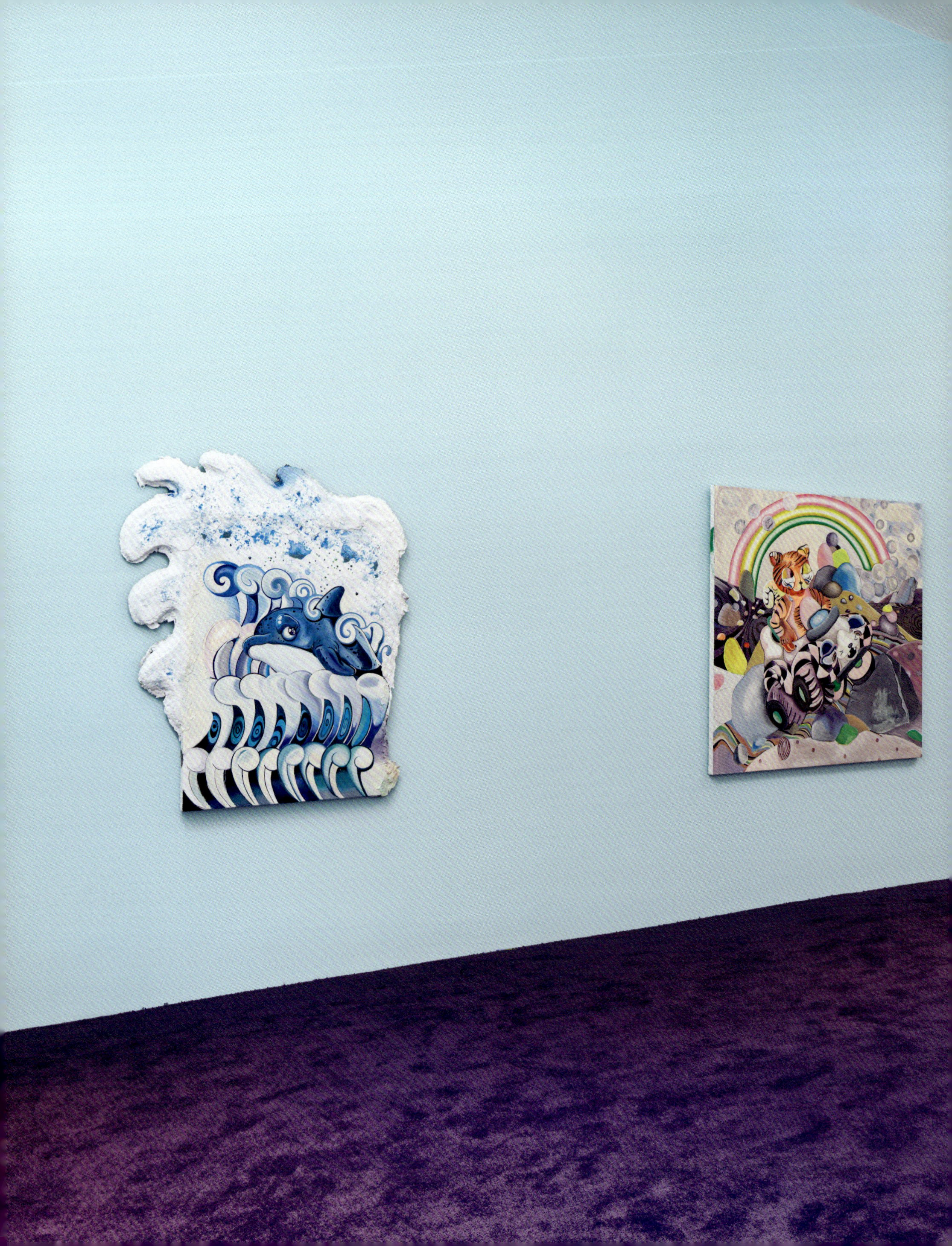

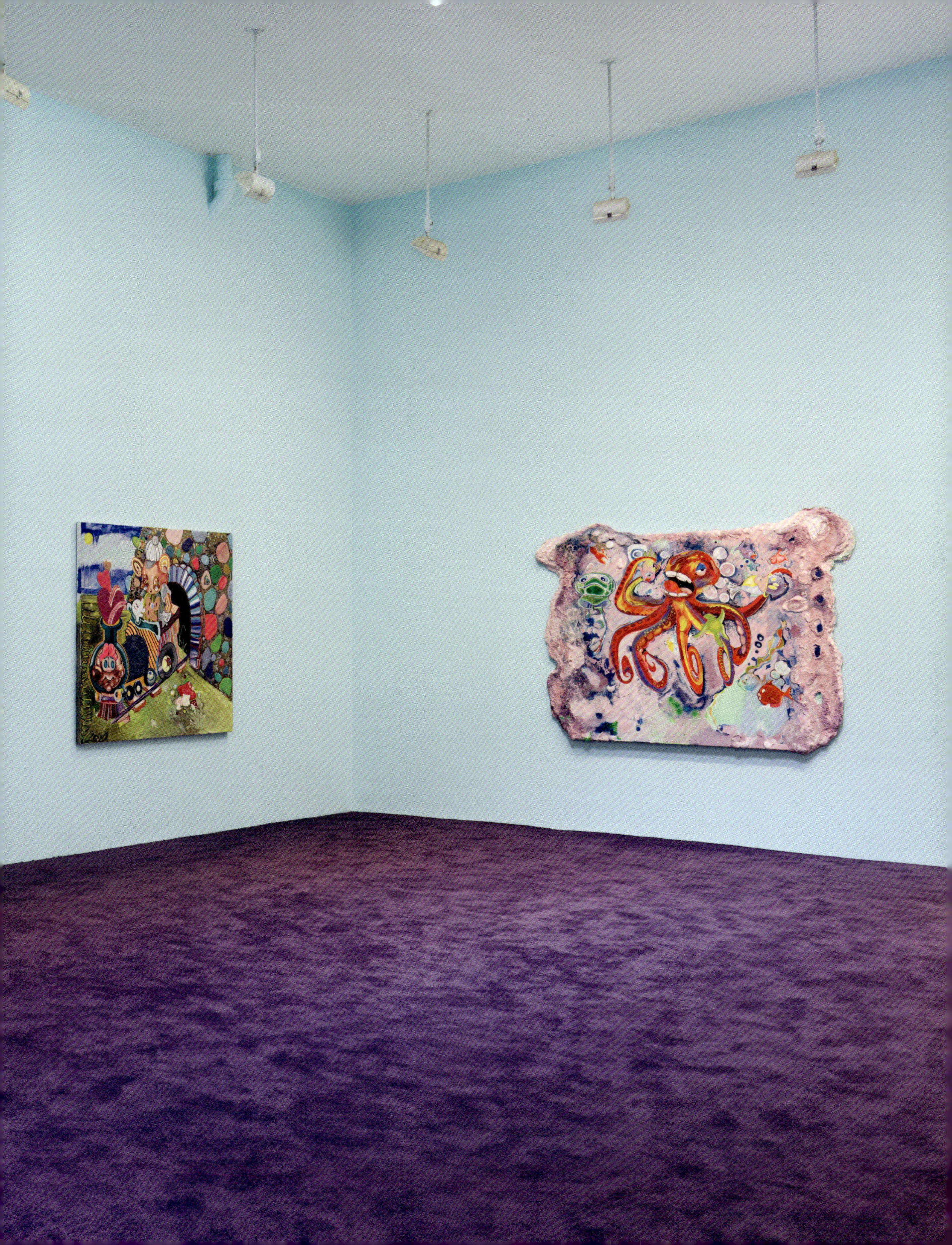

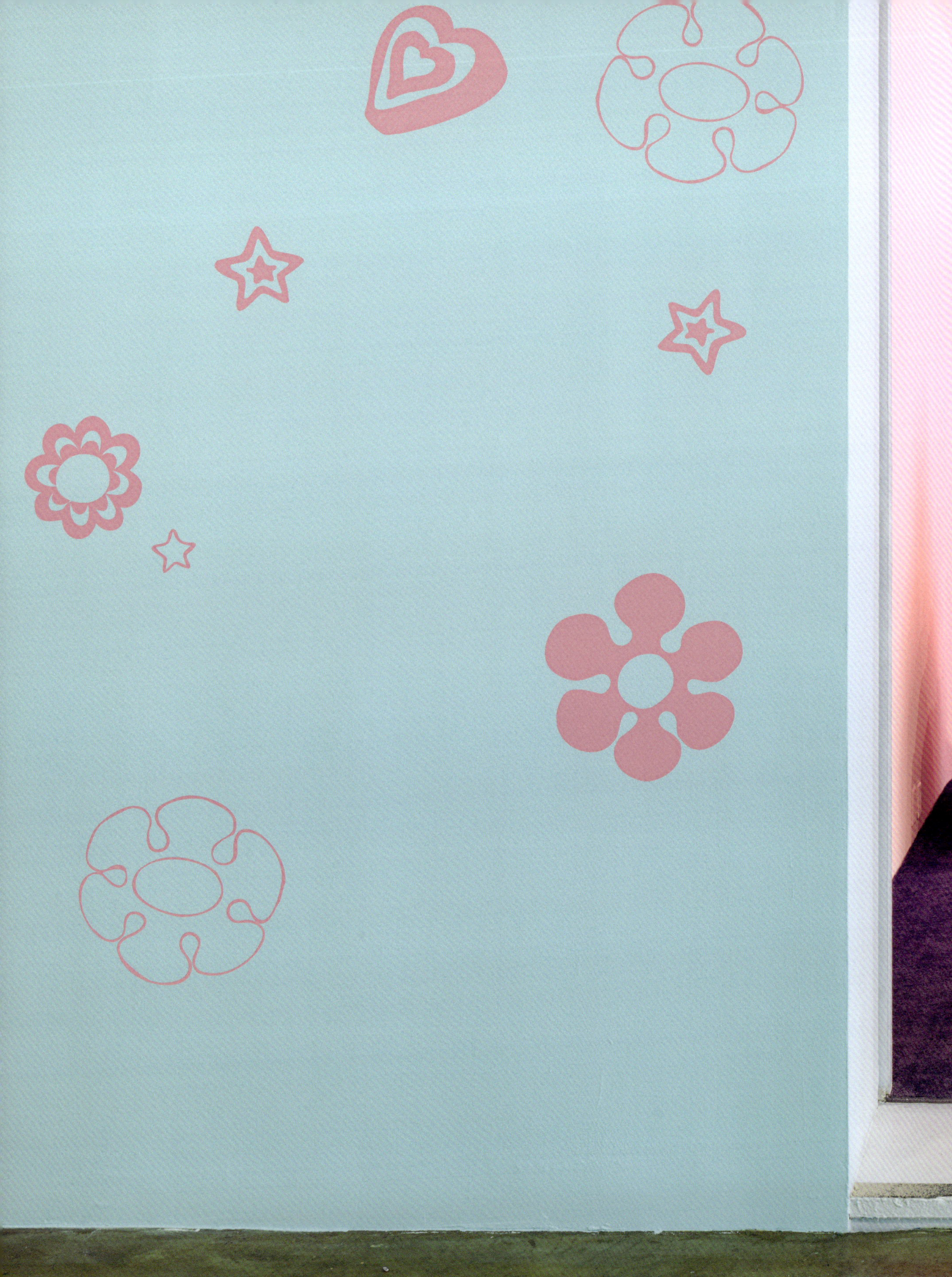

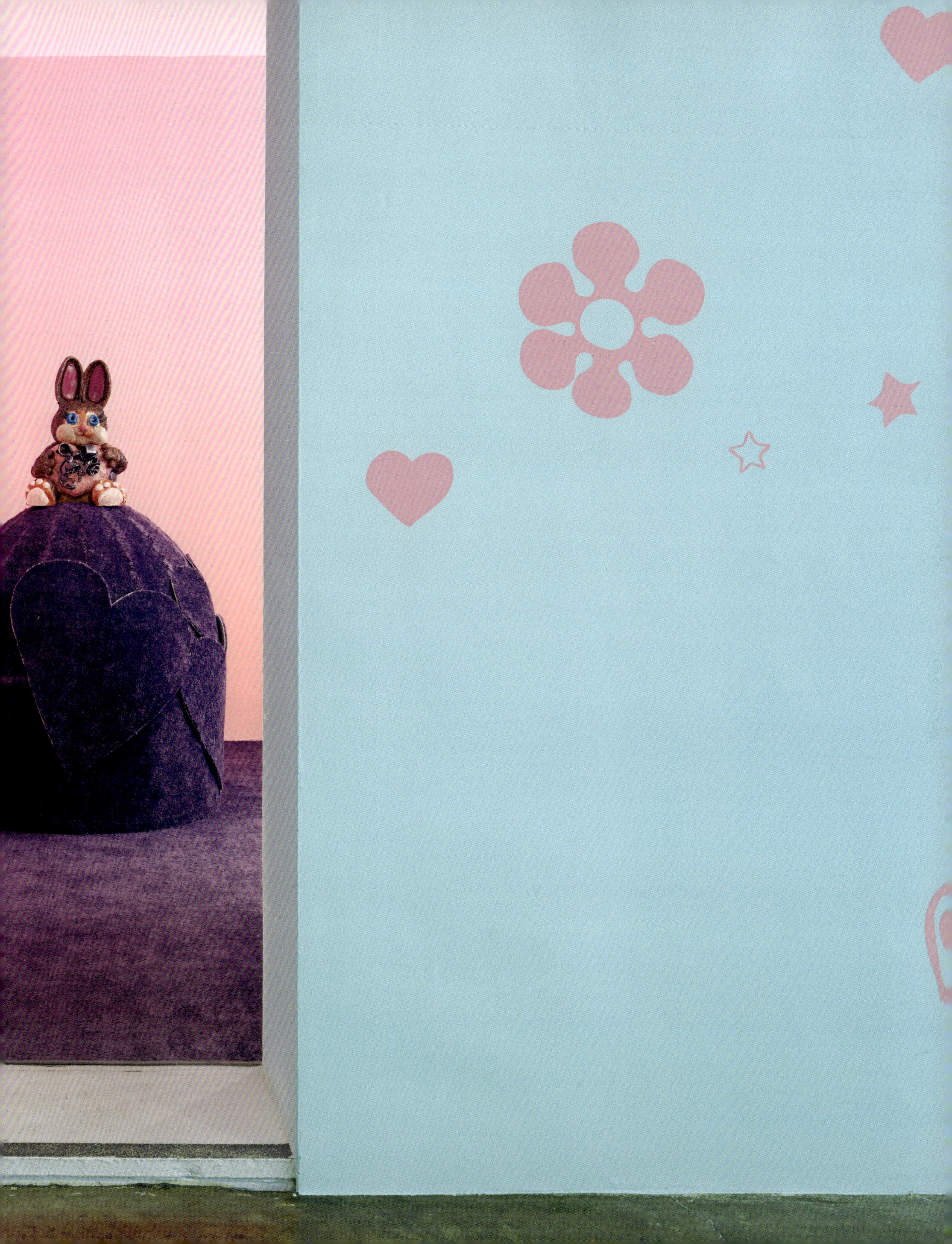

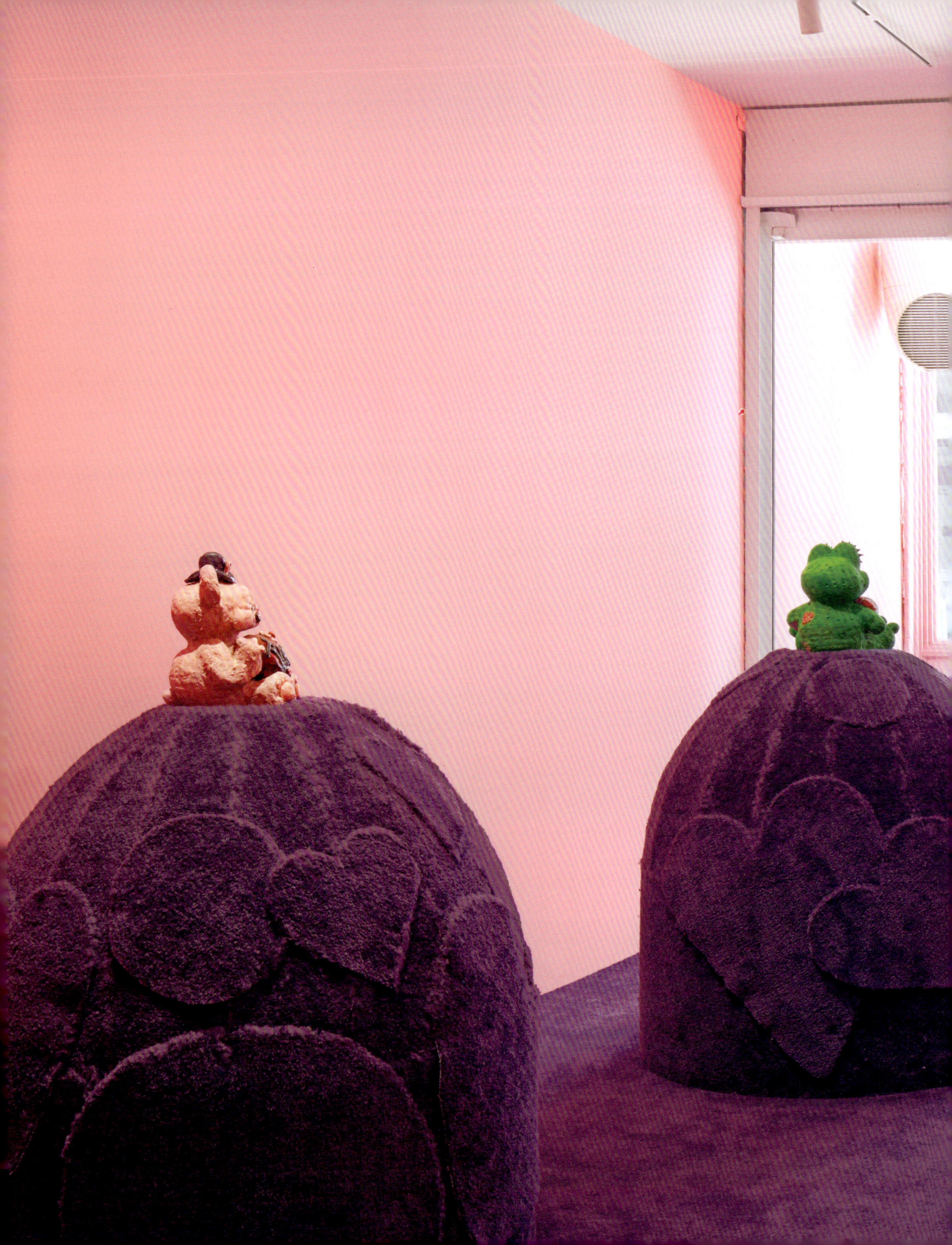

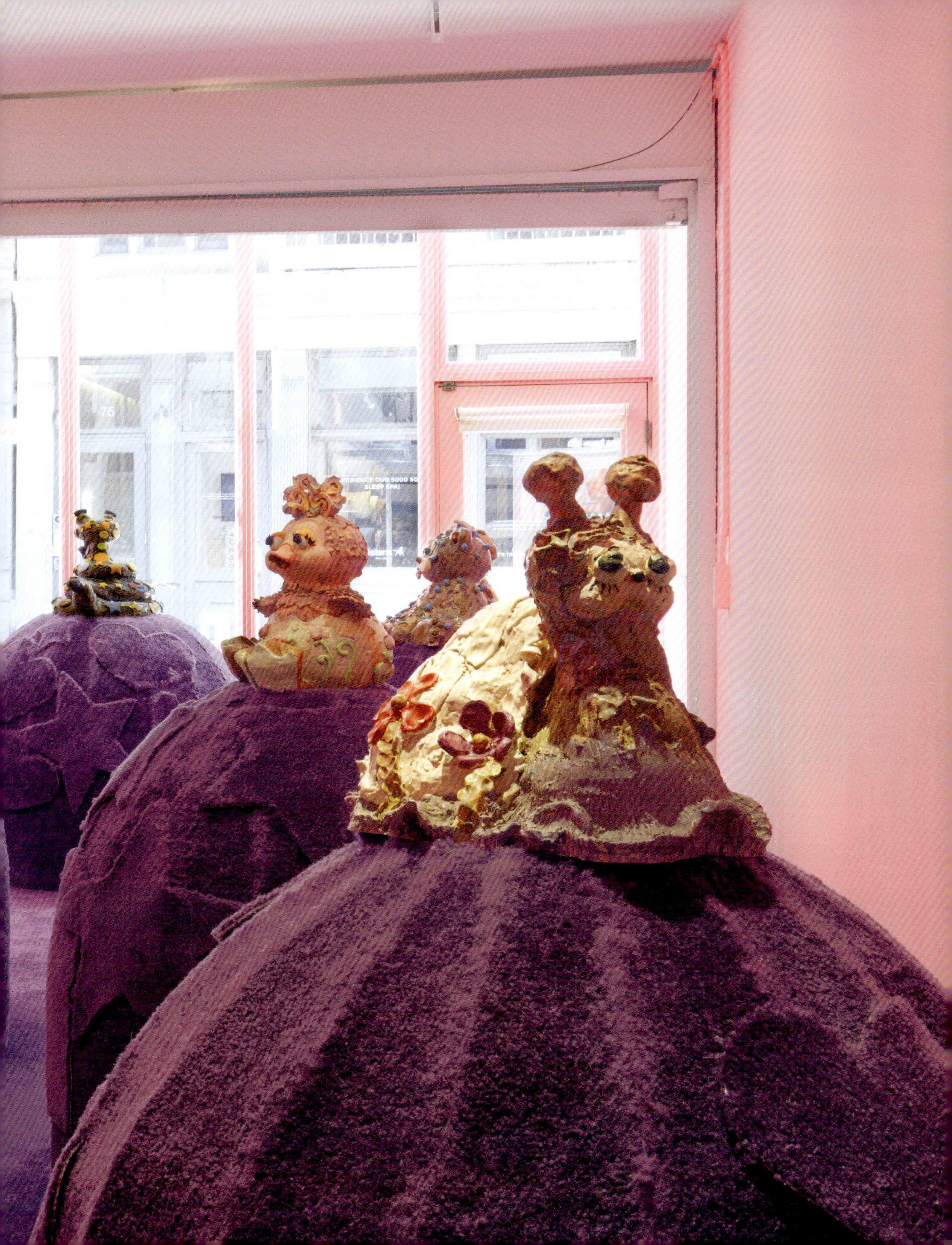

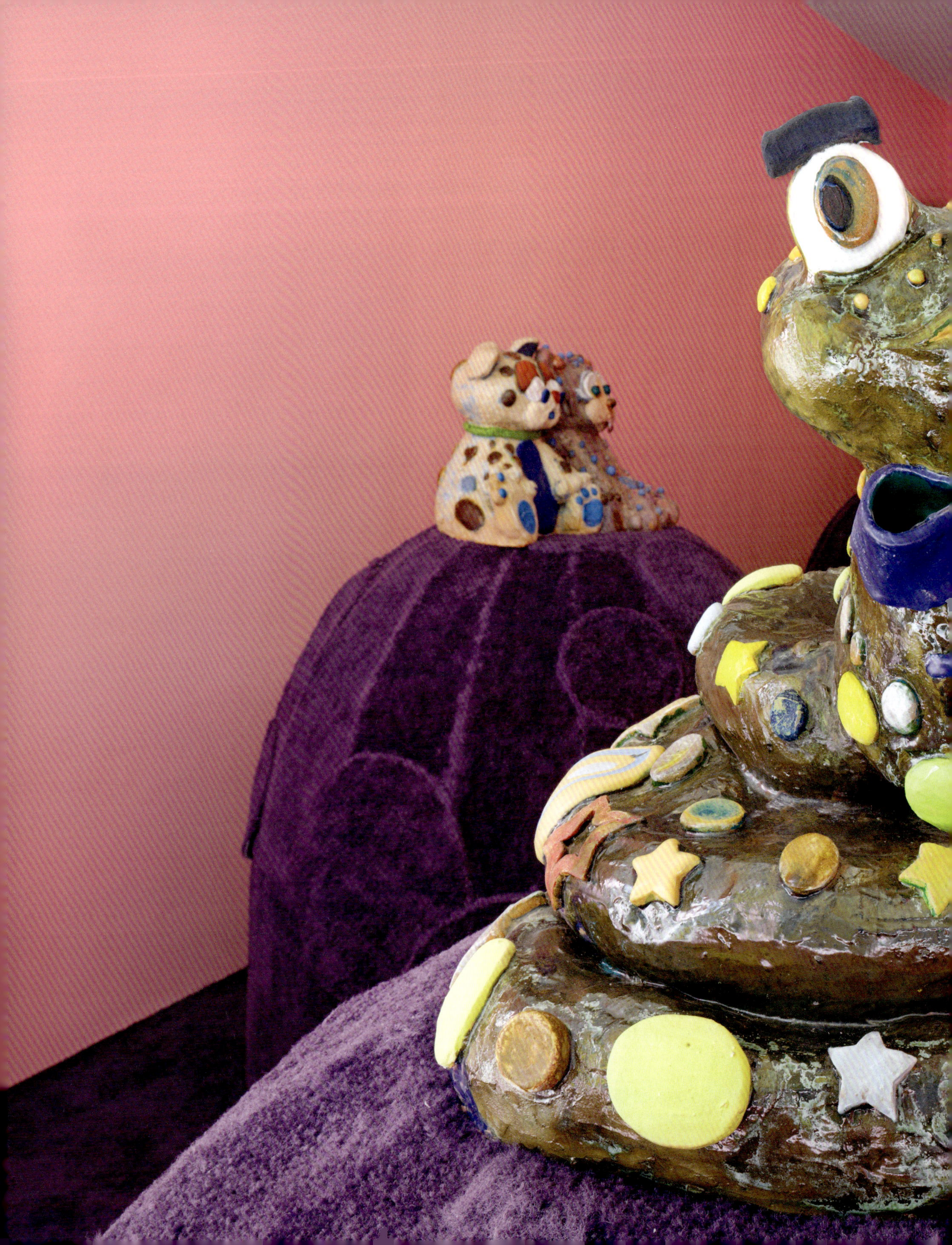

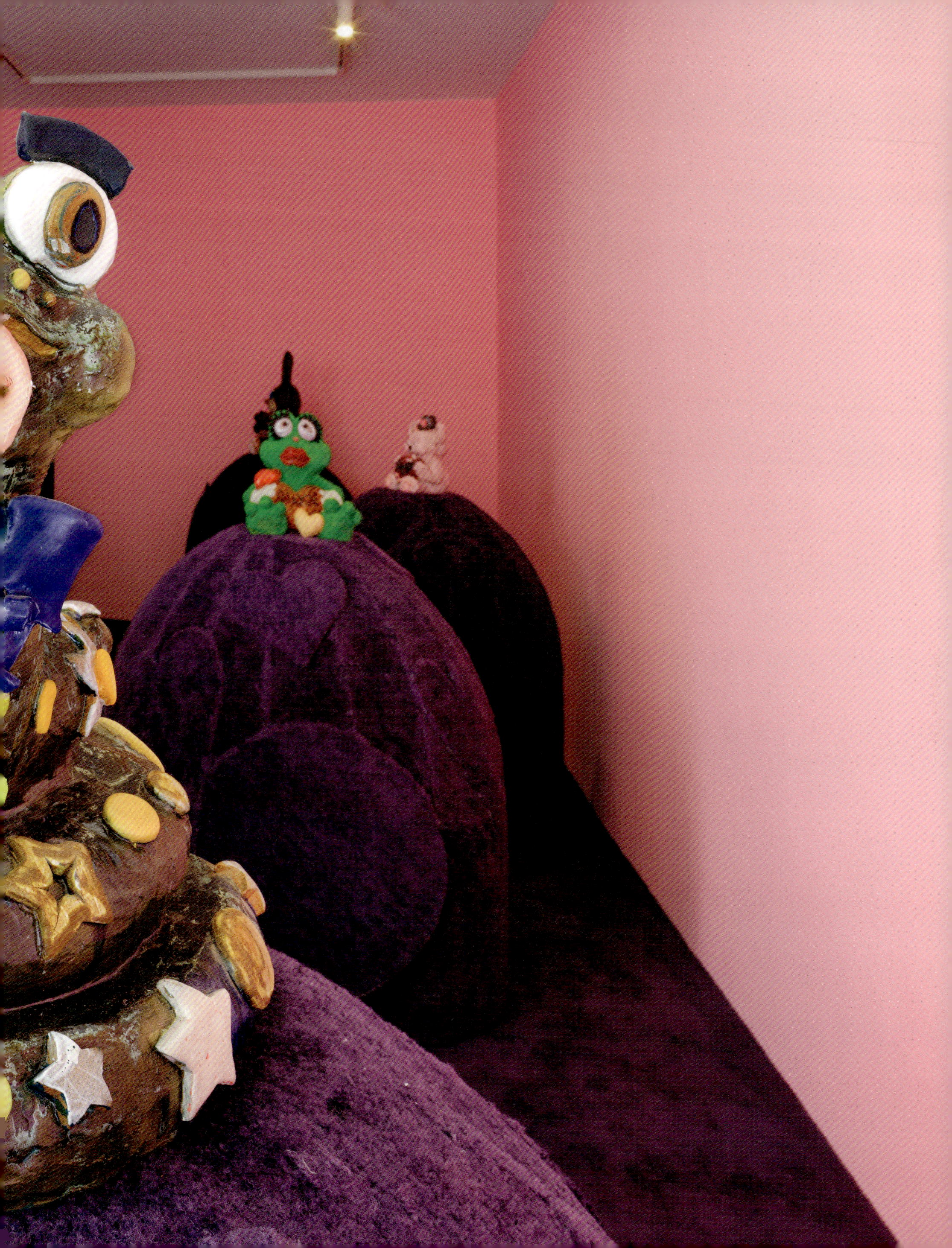

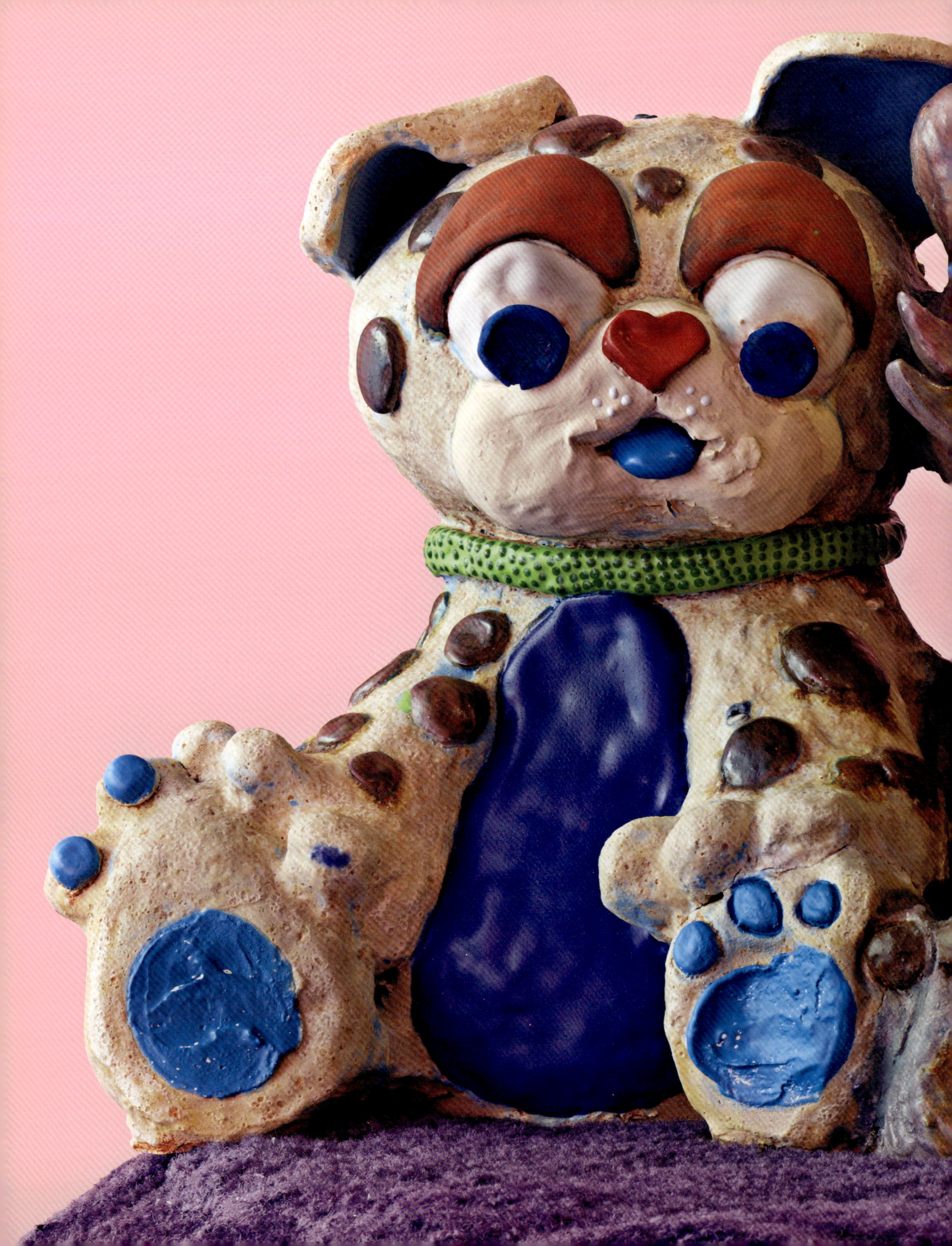

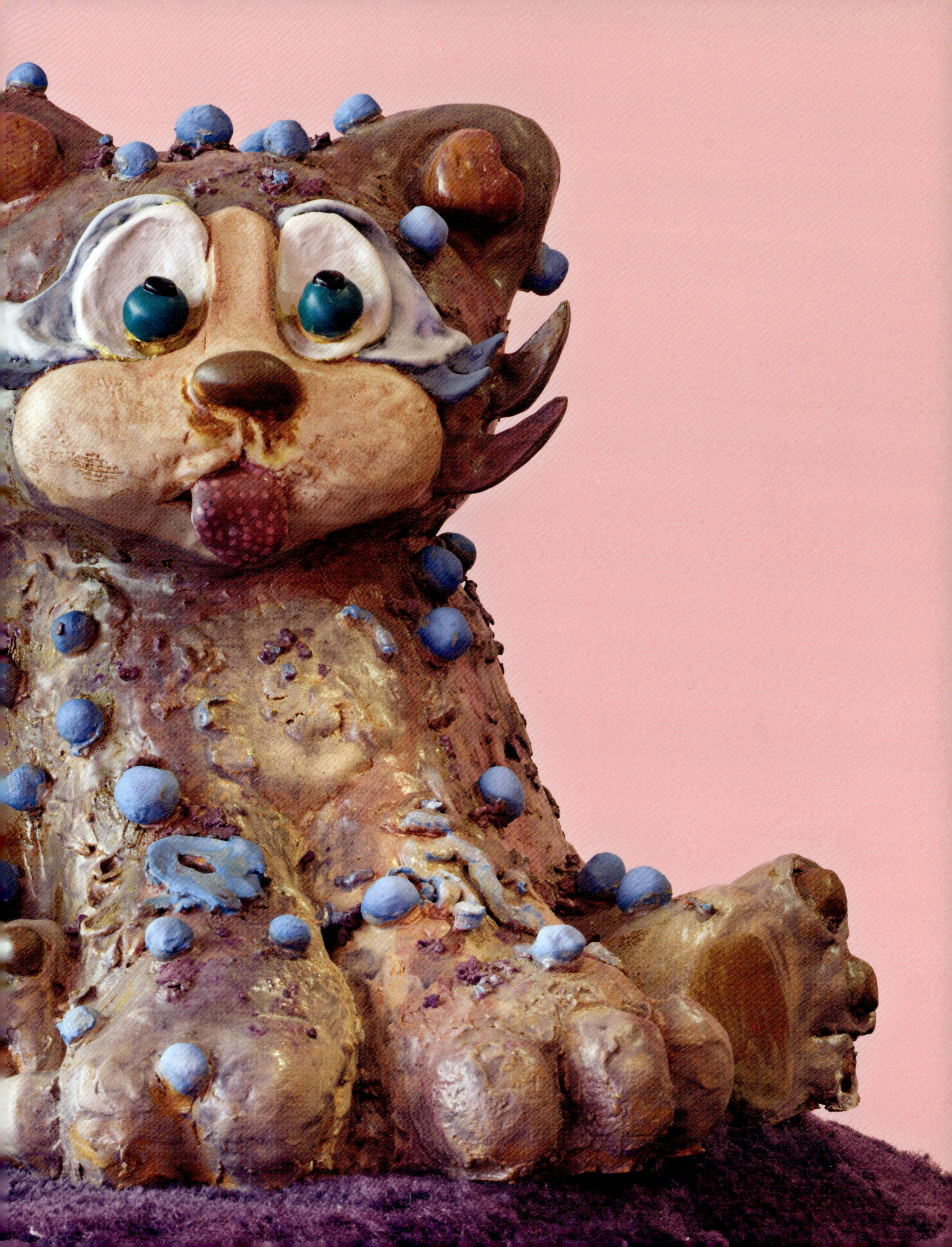

Biography

Alake Shilling was born in 1993 in Los Angeles where continues to live and work. She attended the School of the Art Institute for one year but preferred to forge her own path in the art world. Her most important formative art experience was her internship and exhibition at 356 Mission in Los Angeles, a space for art, performance, and community activities opened in 2012 in the studio of Laura Owens. *The Hippest Trip in America – by Land, Air and Sea*, which opened in the fall of 2021 at Jeffrey Deitch, is Shilling's first solo exhibition in New York.

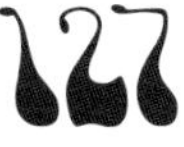

Colophon

This book was published
on the occasion of the exhibition

Alake Shilling
The Hippest Trip in America—by Land, Air and Sea
September 10–October 30, 2021
Jeffrey Deitch
76 Grand Street
New York, NY 10013

Published by Pacific & Jeffrey Deitch, 2023
www.pacificpacific.pub
www.deitch.com

Alake Shilling, Pacific & Jeffrey Deitch

All artwork © Alake Shilling

Texts by Kidogo K. Kennedy, Grant Levy-Lucero, Perwana
Nazif, Laura Owens

Design by Pacific

Artist Liaison: Alia Dahl

Editorial Coordination: Viola Angiolini

Special thanks to Nathan Bennett, Melissa 'Misa' Chhan,
William Croghan, Sharif Farrag, Melahn Frierson, Kathy
Huang Kidogo K. Kennedy, Grant Levy-Lucero, Perwana
Nazif, Laura Owens, Cima Rahmankhah, Darren Romanelli,
Ellery Whaley, Jonas Wood, Wendy Yao.

Printed in Italy

ISBN: 978-1-7375998-2-1

SOURCES: ARTWORK CREDITS

p. 50   Sylvie Fleury, *Palettes of Shadows*, 2018, Instal-
         lation View. Artworks: © Sylvie Fleury. Photo:
         Charles Duprat. Courtesy Thaddaeus Ropac
         Gallery, London·Paris·Salzburg·Seoul

p. 51   Erwin Wurm, *Fat Car* (2002).
         Courtesy the artist and Lehmann Maupin,
         New York, Hong Kong, Seoul, and London

         Chris Martin, *Seven Pointed Star for Isaac Hayes*
         (2008), oil and mixed media on canvas, 64 1/8 × 59
         1/4 inches. Courtesy of David Kordansky Gallery

         Alma Thomas, detail of *A Fantastic Sunset* (1970),
         acrylic on canvas, 48 × 48 inches

         Sarah Canright, *Untitled (Locomotive)* (1966),
         oil on canvas, 27 × 36 inches. Private Collection

p. 53   Brian Belott, *Clock Eyed Cat (Portrait of Bob)* (2003),
         acrylic and glitter on glass in artist's frame, 38 × 49
         inches. Courtesy of the artist and Morán Morán

ALAKE SHILLING: SOLO SHOTS AND INSTALLATION VIEWS PHOTO CREDITS

p. 59   Courtesy of the artist
p. 61   Collection of the Hammer Museum,
            Los Angeles. Puchase.
p. 63   Private Collection. Photo by Joshua White
p. 65-69   Courtesy Rubell Musuem, Miami.
            Photos by Chi Lam
p. 71   Photo curtesy of Salon 94, New York
p. 73   Collection of Jeffrey Deitch.
            Photo by Elon Schoenholz
p. 75   Troy Carter Collection. Photo by Joshua White
p. 77   Photo by Genevieve Hanson
p. 79   Collection of Sarah Hendler and Vinny Dotolo.
            Photo by Genevieve Hanson
p. 81   Collection of Agnes Lew.
            Photo by Genevieve Hanson
p. 83   Troy Carter Collection.
            Photo by Genevieve Hanson
p. 85   Private Collection. Photo by Genevieve Hanson
p. 87   Ariel Emanuel Family Collection.
            Photo by Genevieve Hanson
p. 89   Collection of Ian Skelly.
            Photo by Genevieve Hanson
p. 91   Benny Blanco Collection.
            Photo by Genevieve Hanson
p. 93   Collection of William Leung aka @Willnyc.
            Photo by Genevieve Hanson
p. 95   Collection of the artist.
            Photo by Genevieve Hanson
p. 97   Private Collection of Dr. Michael Glassner and
            Rebecca Creskoff. Photo by Genevieve Hanson
p. 99   Collection of Shio Kusaka and Jonas Wood.
            Photo by Genevieve Hanson
p. 101   Collection of Jeffrey Deitch.
            Photo by Genevieve Hanson
p. 103   Collection of the artist.
            Photo by Genevieve Hanson
pp. 104-125 Installation views by Genevieve Hanson.
            Courtesy of the artist and Jeffrey Deitch,
            New York.